THE MOVIE MAKERS HITCHCOCK

HITCHCOCK

George Perry

M

Front endpaper: Hitchcock
on location in Morocco for
his 1956 remake of *The
Man Who knew Too Much*

Half title page: Hitchcock
with Henry Fonda in *The
Wrong Man*

Title page: Hitchcock in
his native London filming
Frenzy. The opening
sequence used a superb
helicopter shot of the
Thames, ending where
Hitchcock is standing, in
front of County Hall

Back endpaper: Sparrow
strike—a household is
invaded in *The Birds*

© George Perry 1975

SBN 333 17361 9

First published 1975 by
Macmillan London Limited
London and Basingstoke
Associated companies in New York, Toronto,
Dublin, Melbourne, Johannesburg and Delhi

Filmset and printed in Great Britain
by Jolly and Barber Ltd., Rugby
Bound by Dorstel Press Ltd., Harlow

Contents

That he is a master there can be no doubt. He has excelled as no one else in an area of cinema that has become synonymous with his gigantic talent – the suspense thriller. He has built his own shrine at which his imitators can worship. Although most of his films in the past thirty-five years have been American he is far and away the most important director to emerge from the studios of Britain. Alfred Hitchcock made his first film half a century ago; now, near the close of a career of astounding longevity and consistent quality the great imagination is still active and unflagging. Few directors of silent movies in the twenties are remembered by the great mass of filmgoers. Even fewer can still make films.

Hitchcock's extraordinary achievement has been to unite his audiences – on the one hand, the masses in search of anodyne entertainment, the escapist allure of the cinema, and on the other, the intellectuals, film buffs and dedicated cineastes ready to perceive unexpected subtleties in every frame. A Hitchcock film has the advantage of being enjoyable on several levels, and as audiences throughout the world have known for several decades, is invariably superb entertainment.

The French regard Hitchcock as the complete film-maker, the *auteur* to whom no aspect of the filmic structure is a mystery. Every image that appears on the screen has been calculated precisely, from the moulding of the screenplay through the photographic composition to the editing of picture and soundtrack. Even the marketing of the finished product is a major part of Hitchcock's concern, and the gleam in his eye is that of the born showman. His name is known to almost every person who has ever stepped into a cinema, his personality is more familiar than those of many major stars.

Yet how many of his audience know of his early work, particularly the films that are considered too old to be shown on television? How many are aware that he had made his name as long ago as 1926, when his first true suspense thriller, *The Lodger*, was released? How many appreciate that almost every innovation in the cinema – including the many trendy artifices of fashionable young directors in recent years, such as jump-cutting, overlapping sound, freeze frames, slowed-down action – was anticipated years earlier by Hitchcock?

As François Truffaut, the brilliant French director and devoted Hitchcock admirer, has pointed out, when a film-maker sets out to make a Western he is not necessarily thinking of John Ford, since Howard Hawks and Raoul Walsh made equally fine films in this genre. But when he makes a thriller or a suspense picture then you can be certain that he is hoping to turn out something that can be compared with one of Hitchcock's masterpieces.

He is, therefore, one of the cinema's great original forces.

Minneapolis, April 1974

Hitchcock on location in a London street during the filming of *Stage Fright*

1899-1927

Mᴿ HITCHCOCK

The north-eastern suburb of Leyton is a typical London district – densely built over with redbrick villas and high-rise council flats; the main roads are congested with shoppers and traffic. But, at the turn of the century, the affinity with the rural Essex hinterland was still visible, as it had only lately been encroached upon by the expanding Victorian metropolis. It was in this place that Alfred Joseph Hitchcock was born, on 13 August 1899, a scion of the burgeoning lower middle classes.

His father was a shopowner, a purveyor of poultry and vegetables. He was also a Catholic. That fact was to have a marked effect on his son's upbringing. At an early age little Alfred went off to St Ignatius College, a Jesuit boarding school. But before that day came he had undergone what was to be the most famous incident of his childhood, and which he has always claimed had a lasting influence on his outlook and work. His father had punished him for some forgotten offence by sending him with a note to the local police station. The sergeant, a friend of his father, read it and promptly locked the young boy, then only four or five years old, in a cell for a few minutes, with the words: 'That's what we do with naughty little boys!' These moments of unjust custody were not to be forgotten, and fear of incarceration is a recurring theme in his films.

The boy Hitchcock was no delinquent. He was quiet, shy, studious and well behaved. He was not renowned for his prowess at team games, preferring to watch others rather than participate himself. The Jesuit education was strict, its intellectual disciplines exacting, and it was from the priests that he learned the use of willpower to achieve methodical organization. He also developed at their hands a strong awareness of the force of evil and a sense of moral fear. He was an above-average pupil, and geography was his best subject. As an example of his curiosity for exploring places he had even fulfilled a private ambition by travelling along every route of the London General Omnibus Company, thus seeing every district in London.

Engineering attracted him and after leaving school he trained for a brief period at a specialized college. He then joined the cable-making company, W. T. Henley, and by the age of nineteen had become a technical estimator. But another side of his character was also beginning to develop. He had enrolled in a fine arts course at London University and was now showing considerable interest in graphics. His caricatures of staff members in the Henley house magazine were greatly admired and soon he was transferred from the drawing office to the advertising department, where he became a layout man.

It was now that the cinema began to beckon him in earnest. His parents had been avid theatregoers, but the youthful Hitchcock had exercised a preference for the unsteady

Ivor Novello, mysteriously garbed, makes a nocturnal foray from a Bloomsbury boarding house in *The Lodger*: behaviour that eventually makes him a murder suspect

flickerings of the silent screen. He revelled in a diet of Chaplin, Keaton, Fairbanks, Pickford and Griffith, and the latter's *Birth of a Nation* and *Intolerance* made a profound impression. He amused himself designing title cards for some of the films he had seen, and then it occurred to him that if only the studios could see his work he could earn money. He read the trade press and hopefully began banging on the doors of Wardour Street. He learned that the American company of Famous Players-Lasky was establishing production in London, and on approaching them found to his great delight that he was hired.

A silent picture required anything up to a couple of hundred inserted title cards to provide dialogue or narrative. During the twenties these cards had become progressively more decorative, embellishing the cliché-ridden words with visual devices to hammer the point home. Quite often Hitchcock's work involved rewriting dialogue to make a film more acceptable to its audience. The silent cinema was astonishingly flexible and it was possible to turn a poor drama into a sparkling comedy simply by providing new titles. During this period Hitchcock was to learn how films were assembled, and, perhaps more to the point, how they could be reassembled.

The ambitious youth became totally absorbed in the cinema. He even made a tentative attempt at directing a picture called *Number Thirteen*, which was to star Clare Greet. But the Americans withdrew from the studio and the project was abandoned. He was then asked by Seymour Hicks to finish off with him a film of one of his plays on which the original director had dropped out. The completed film was *Always Tell Your Wife*. Hitchcock had now attracted the attention of a young advertising film producer from Birmingham, Michael Balcon, who had gone into feature film production in association with Victor Saville and Graham Cutts. Cutts was to direct *Woman to Woman* and Betty Compson was brought over from Hollywood to star in it at the then astronomical salary for the British film industry of £1000 per week. Hitchcock was the assistant director, script collaborator and art director – a range of functions that one man would find virtually impossible to encompass nowadays. The resulting film was a great success and the leading man, Clive Brook, got a Hollywood contract on the strength of it. The film was edited by the script girl – a not uncommon combination of roles in those days – who was Alma Reville. Later, after a two-year engagement she became Mrs Alfred Hitchcock.

The successful Balcon team went on to make *The White Shadow* and under the aegis of the newly-formed company, Gainsborough, *The Passionate Adventure*, which Hitchcock wrote. It was now 1925 and the British film industry was undergoing one of its periodic recessions. Balcon made a deal with the chief of UFA in Germany, Erich Pommer, to make

married

Above: Betty Compson (left) in *Woman to Woman*, directed by Graham Cutts in 1922. Hitchcock was assistant director, co-screenwriter and art director

Below: *The White Shadow*, with Betty Compson (centre), was the 1923 follow-up with the same teamwork of Cutts and Hitchcock

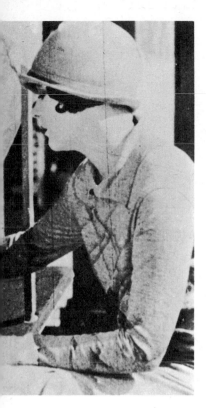

Above: The first film wholly directed by Hitchcock was *The Pleasure Garden* (1925). John Stewart is soothed by Virginia Valli

Above left: *The Blackguard* with Walter Rilla and Jane Novak, with art direction and screenplay by Hitchcock

Left: Clive Brook and Lillian Hall-Davies in *The Passionate Adventure*, the first film from the Gainsborough company

three films in that country. The first, *The Blackguard*, with Jane Novak and Walter Rilla, was made at the Neubabelsberg Studios, with Graham Cutts directing, and Hitchcock assisting, designing and screenwriting. He performed the same functions on another film, this time made at home, at the Gainsborough Studios in Islington. It was called *The Prude's Fall*. Cutts had now decided that he did not want Hitchcock working with him any longer, probably suspecting that the young man was becoming a threat. Michael Balcon stepped in, and with his perception of outstanding talent that was to characterize his long contribution to British films, he decided to make the 25-year-old a director in his own right.

The first film Hitchcock wholly directed was another Anglo-German production, made at the Emelka Studios in Munich. Pursuing his policy of securing Hollywood stars to attract the American market, Balcon had signed Virginia Valli and Carmelita Geraghty for leading roles, and a third American actress, Nita Naldi, for a smaller part. The story of *The Pleasure Garden* was melodramatic and trite. It was about two chorus girls at the Pleasure Garden Theatre, one with a fiancé stationed in the Tropics to whom she is indifferent. The other marries a man on leave from the same colony and spends an idyllically photographed honeymoon on Lake Como. The husband returns to his outpost and philanders with a native girl who kills herself when the wife arrives. He attempts to murder her but is shot down by the local doctor. The wife, now widowed, nurses her friend's ex-fiancé through a fever and presumably they live happily ever after. In spite of the inherent absurdity of the tale the film had a distinctive glossy style. The cameraman, Baron Ventimiglia, although Italian had worked extensively with American directors whom Hitchcock was anxious to emulate, having also studied their techniques. It was a sufficiently auspicious directorial debut for the *Daily Express* to hail him as an outstandingly promising newcomer.

The second film was also made at Emelka and on location in the Austrian Tyrol. Regrettably no print of it is known to have survived and it is the only film from Hitchcock's large output to have sunk totally without trace. Like *The Pleasure Garden* the screenplay was again by Eliot Stannard and Ventimiglia was the cameraman. Nita Naldi played the part of a village schoolmistress taking refuge in the mountains of Kentucky after being driven out because of allegedly wanton behaviour. A mysterious hermit, played by Malcolm Keen, rescues her. Hitchcock speaks disparagingly of the film, and resented the casting of Naldi, which was forced on him in order to secure adequate distribution in the United States. *The Mountain Eagle* was the last film Balcon produced in Germany, although he and Pommer continued an association until the rise of Hitler in the thirties.

The third film that Hitchcock made was the first in the genre
with which he would forevermore be associated – the suspense
thriller. The story was adapted by Eliot Stannard from a brilliant novel by Mrs Belloc-Lowndes based on a Jack-the-Ripper
theme, in which an unknown murderer is at large eliminating
blondes. To a Bloomsbury boarding house comes a mysterious young man who keeps himself to himself and paces the
floor despairingly before gliding out of the house on nocturnal
sorties. Inevitably he is suspected, arrested and all but lynched
before his innocence is established by the capture of the real
killer in the very act. A major figure from the West End stage
was cast in the lead, the popular Ivor Novello. The fact that he
was a matinee idol meant that he had to be found innocent at
the end, much to Hitchcock's disappointment, for he would
have preferred to have left open the possibility that he was the
murderer. The same problem would crop up years later when
Cary Grant behaved like a murder suspect in *Suspicion*.

Nevertheless, *The Lodger* vividly demonstrated some recur-

Ivor Novello and June in
The Lodger, Hitchcock's
third film and his first
suspense thriller

– locked up
yet innocent
child hood
fears.

14

June shows off a dress to her parents, Arthur Chesney and Marie Ault, lodging-house keepers in *The Lodger*. All London is agog at a series of murders of golden-haired girls— will June be the next victim?

ring Hitchcock themes – the cumulation of circumstantial evidence to place an innocent man in serious jeopardy, the hysterical unreason of the mob, even the use of handcuffs, presaging a prop used in several later films such as *The Thirty Nine Steps*, *Saboteur* and *The Wrong Man*. It was also the first film in which Hitchcock made a tiny appearance – in fact in *The Lodger* he can be seen twice, in a newspaper office and at the end of the film in the crowd witnessing the arrest of Novello. Appearing originally because there was a need to swell the number of extras in this film, Hitchcock later adopted these token glimpses as a 'signature', supposedly offering some assuaging of superstition as well as being a means of exercising his ingenuity in such sparsely peopled films as *Rope* and *Lifeboat*.

When *The Lodger* was completed it was edited by Ivor Montagu, then a film critic (it is astonishing by today's standards how lightly various specialized functions in film-making were tossed around in the flexible twenties), and the poster

15

artist McKnight Kauffer designed the titles, which had also been written with considerable economy by Montagu. The distributors then sat through a preview of the film, decided that it was too heavy in treatment, obscure in plot and gloomy of theme to do anything at the box office, and accordingly shelved it. Some months passed before it was decided to risk releasing it. *The Lodger* was acclaimed as one of the best British films ever made and was a huge success with critics and public alike. Hitchcock's reputation was now established at the age of twenty-seven. The film was rich in visual effects that portended the extent of Hitchcock's cinematic imagination. One of the most famous was the glass ceiling, whereby the man pacing upstairs became visible from the room below. Such devices were more necessary in the silent cinema; sound made it possible to convey information more succinctly.

In spite of offers from America to work there, Hitchcock remained with Balcon at Islington. Ivor Novello was to be his star again in a story partly of his own authorship, although Eliot Stannard was once more the screenwriter. *Downhill* was about a schoolboy expelled after a false accusation of theft and disowned by an overbearing father. He drifts through various adventures, marries a worthless actress who cheats him of all his money, becomes a gigolo and after years of going down the drain loses his health. Restored to England and his family, he learns that his name has been cleared. The novelettishness of the story proved impossible for Hitchcock to surmount. There were, however, one or two interesting scenes, in particular a dream sequence shot without dissolves so that reality transformed into hallucination without any blurred edges, but the film was a disappointment after its much better predecessor.

Nor was the next much of an improvement. It was *Easy Virtue*, adapted from the play by Noel Coward. Somehow the translation of his brittle flow of dialogue into silent film subtitles so lessened the dramatic effect that the emptiness of the plot showed through. It was an attempt at social comment, showing the consequences of a blinkered attitude towards divorce. Isabel Jeans, who had played the actress in *Downhill*, was now cast as Laurita, a woman who divorces her drunken husband and remarries without revealing to her new spouse her former marital history. When the family eventually find out she is again divorced and her life ruined. These two films, *Downhill* and *Easy Virtue*, were routine assignments, awarded to Hitchcock simply because of his availability, and not because there was anything in either of them that suited his style. But in spite of their relative failures *The Lodger* had established him as the most promising young film director, and he was able to command the colossal salary, by prevailing standards, of £15,000 a year. Hitchcock needed a change of studio, and so he accepted an offer from John Maxwell at British International Pictures, Elstree.

Above: Ivor Novello is confronted by his accuser in the headmaster's study in *Downhill*

Below: Isabel Jeans and Robin Irvine in *Easy Virtue*, an unsuccessful adaptation of Noel Coward's play

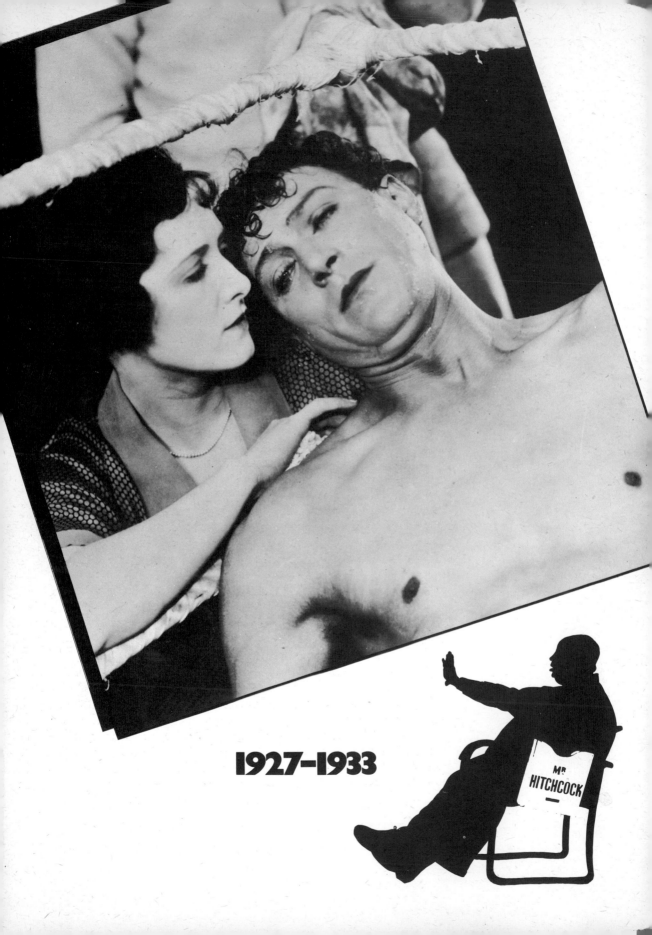

1927-1933

The Ring was the first of the films to be made at the new studios, and the script was by Hitchcock himself. An original screenplay, it was about two boxers in love with the same girl. The title refers not only to the fight arena, but also to a serpentine bracelet which appears in several sequences, and stands as a symbol of faithlessness. Carl Brisson played the hero, Ian Hunter his smooth adversary and Lillian Hall-Davies the girl. In a small part as the trainer was Gordon Harker, making an effective comic debut. The opening of the film took place in a fairground boxing booth. The hero was known as 'One Round' Jack, since no challenger could last beyond the first round. That he had met his mark was shown by the worn, shabby card on a stand with the figure '1' on it, replaced by a shiny, new sign '2'. In another scene the young boxer returns home from winning a fight, and jubilantly pours out champagne for his friends. He then learns that his wife is out with the other man. There is a shot of the champagne in the glasses visibly going flat.

Though well-received by the critics, The Ring was not unfortunately a commercial success. Yet after The Lodger it is the best of his silent output. To follow it Hitchcock turned to a well-known stage success, adapting Eden Philpott's long-running rustic comedy, The Farmer's Wife. The plot concerned the efforts of a middle-aged widower to find a new wife among the available females in the district, yet overlooking until the last reel the obvious and logical attractions of his devoted housekeeper. It was hardly the most satisfactory material for Hitchcock's style, and apart from Gordon Harker's impact as a farmhand, a comic role he invested with characteristic good humour, the film had little to commend it. Jack Cox photographed some pleasing exteriors, but the moment the film moved indoors it was swamped with titles, its stage origins clearly manifest.

Eliot Stannard renewed his collaboration with Hitchcock on the next film, Champagne. It is a film that Hitchcock himself despises, although it is not as bad as he claims. Betty Balfour, who had become prominent in George Pearson's Squibs series, played an heiress told by her father, who objects to her fiancé, that their family had been ruined. She gets a job in a cabaret selling the family commodity – champagne. Eventually her father relents and permits her to marry the man of her choice. The most effective sequence was on board ship in mid-ocean, with Betty Balfour landing alongside in a seaplane, her leather aviatrix outfit in marked contrast with the pearls and satin décolleté of the shipboard passengers. 'We ended up with a hodge-podge of a story that was written as we went through the film, and I thought it was dreadful,' said Hitchcock.

The Manxman was his last silent work, made in 1929 when the new talking pictures were becoming established. Eliot

Lillian Hall-Davies whispers encouragement to a battered Carl Brisson during a tense break in a decisive battle in The Ring

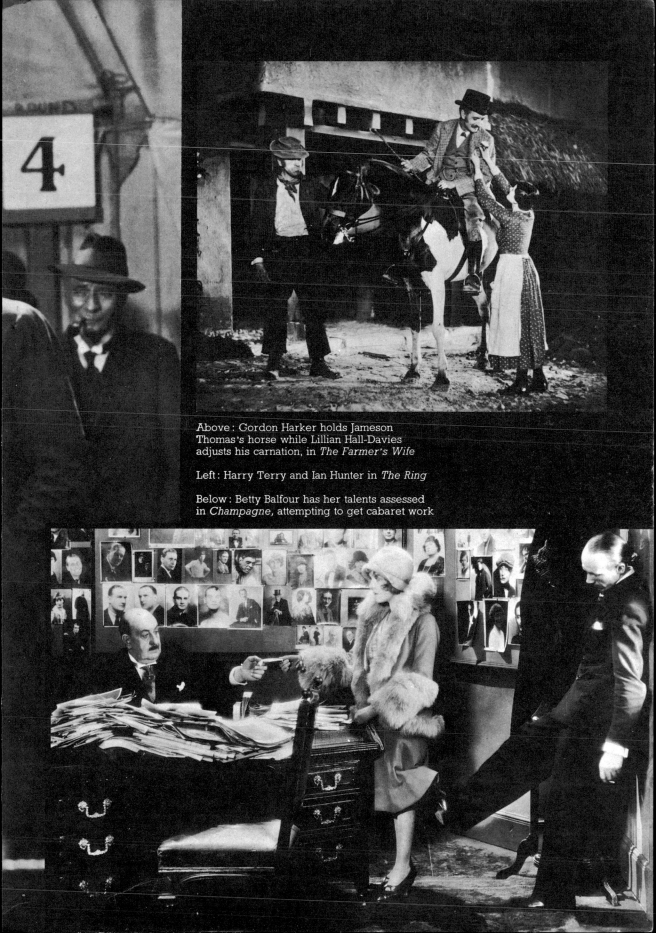

Above: Gordon Harker holds Jameson
Thomas's horse while Lillian Hall-Davies
adjusts his carnation, in *The Farmer's Wife*

Left: Harry Terry and Ian Hunter in *The Ring*

Below: Betty Balfour has her talents assessed
in *Champagne*, attempting to get cabaret work

Stannard adapted the screenplay from the long romantic novel by Hall Caine. In it Carl Brisson played a fisherman and Malcolm Keen a young lawyer, both in love with the same girl in their village on the Isle of Man, who was played by the beautiful blonde Czechoslovakian actress, Anny Ondra. After the fisherman is reported drowned the lawyer declares his love and they have an affair. Then the first lover reappears, and bound by her old promise she marries him, even though she is now pregnant by the second man. She tries to kill herself, a punishable offence under Manx law, and she is brought to trial. Her lawyer lover is on the tribunal, and after a public confession he throws up his career to take the girl and her new-born child away from the island. In spite of Jack Cox's stylish photography the story could barely rise above the mawkishness of its concept, and it was a disappointing conclusion to Hitchcock's silent period. In fact the film was not released until January 1930, two months after his first talkie had been seen by the public. But with Anny Ondra Hitchcock had begun his fascination for the ice-cool blonde, whose outward poise concealed rampant sexuality.

Talking pictures caught on when Warner Brothers in Hollywood decided to take a chance on the Vitaphone process, a sound-on-disc system developed jointly by Western Electric and American Telephone and Telegraph. *The Jazz Singer* with Al Jolson opened at London's Piccadilly Theatre in 1928,

Above: Anny Ondra, the Czech actress who starred in *The Manxman*

Left: Anny Ondra with Carl Brisson. The film was evocatively photographed by Jack Cox

Below: Randle Ayrton, Clare Greet, Malcolm Keen, Carl Brisson in another scene

and immediately began breaking records. Its success plunged the British film industry into panic, as most producers had not regarded sound films as anything more than a passing fad.

Meanwhile Hitchcock had chosen a play by Charles Bennett to turn into a film, and the screenplay was fashioned by them both, with the help of Benn W. Levy. *Blackmail* was a thriller in the familiar Hitchcock vein, territory in which he was happier to work. It was made as a silent picture, although Hitchcock correctly anticipated that before it was completed he would be put under pressure from the front office to release it as a part-talkie, a hybrid type of film extant in the early days of sound, in which the last reel suddenly came alive with voices instead of titles. By advance preparation Hitchcock was able to argue that the film would be far more effective released as a full talkie, and that any reshooting would be minimal. That in fact is what happened.

Anny Ondra, who played the lead, could only speak English with a very heavy accent, which meant that her lines had to be dubbed by a British actress, Joan Barry. Techniques in the early days were very primitive, and the only way it could be done was to have Miss Barry physically present on the set out of camera range, speaking the lines as Ondra on camera mouthed them silently.

Blackmail was about a detective's fiancée who in self-defence kills an artist who has attempted to rape her. Her lover is assigned to the case, and learns of her involvement after a blackmailer who saw her leave the studio has threatened to expose her. The detective adroitly manages to switch suspicion to the blackmailer, who after a spectacular chase through the British Museum falls to his death from the domed roof of the Reading Room. Falls from a great height recur in Hitchcock films, as in *Jamaica Inn, Saboteur, Vertigo* and others, while the use of famous landmarks for the background of chases is another staple element.

For box-office reasons he was denied the ending he wanted. The girl, not the blackmailer, was to have been the police quarry, and the detective was to have had the ironic task of locking her up. An older colleague was to ask as he went off duty: 'Going out with your girl tonight?' and he would have answered, 'No, not tonight!'

In spite of the untried novelty of sound Hitchcock was ready to experiment with the new medium. The scene where a garrulous neighbour, discussing the murder across a breakfast table, harps on the word 'knife' until it is the only word that the girl can hear, is often cited as one of the first uses of impressionistic sound. The first British all-talkie to be released, *Blackmail* drew in the crowds. The clapperboy on the film was the future director Ronald Neame, while another latent major talent, Michael Powell, fulfilled the job of stills cameraman.

Following *Blackmail* Hitchcock was called upon to direct a couple of scenes in *Elstree Calling*, a film revue, imitating the style of the early American musical, which used the medium of sound to present a series of acts taken in many cases direct from the variety and musical comedy stage. Hitchcock's contribution to this ponderous portmanteau work, which claimed to be the first British screen musical, was a couple of sketches featuring Gordon Harker. There was, however, nothing of significance in them.

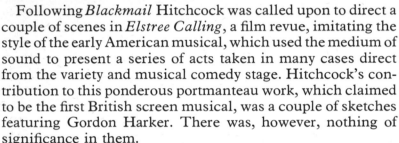

Left: An early personal appearance by Hitchcock in *Blackmail,* as a pestered passenger on an underground train

Above: A scene from the same film, when Anny Ondra realizes that she has just killed her attacker

He then filmed Sean O'Casey's magnificent play, *Juno and the Paycock*, adapting it in association with his wife, Alma Reville. It was a straightforward version of the play, 'filmed theatre' according to Hitchcock, who had qualms in dealing with the material, fearing that desecration would ensue were he to tamper too much with the original. Sara Allgood was cast as Juno, the practical wife of the dreamer, 'Captain' Boyle – the Paycock – who was played by the then virtually unknown actor Edward Chapman. The film received excellent notices, although Hitchcock felt that the respectable literary antecedents of the piece had influenced the critics, rather than the film's minimal cinematic qualities. Chapman's reputation was made with the film and he went on to a long career as an actor. To some extent, in its use of the Dublin background and Irish players the film anticipated John Ford's *The Informer* and his less impressive *The Plough and the Stars*. O'Casey, impressed with the successful reception of *Juno and the Paycock*, put up a suggestion to Hitchcock of a story about Hyde Park. Hitchcock gave his assent and O'Casey went ahead and prepared a script, *Within the Gates*. It was never filmed, but it did become one of O'Casey's lesser stage plays.

Alma Reville then adapted a play called *Enter Sir John* by Clemence Dane and Helen Simpson for the third full-length talkie. Retitled *Murder*, it marked a return to the thriller idiom.

Above: Norah Baring in
the condemned cell in
Murder. The plight of the
innocent in jail is a
recurring Hitchcock theme

Below: Sara Allgood and
Kathleen O'Regan in
Juno and the Paycock

It concerned a young actress in a touring company who was convicted and sentenced to death for the murder of a woman. One juror, coincidentally an actor, but of a rather grand theatrical manner, convinced that the girl was innocent, returned to the touring company and the scene of the crime, in an attempt to unravel the mystery. Eventually the real killer is unmasked in a circus. He is the girl's fiancé, who it happens is also a transvestite trapeze artist.

The plot, melodramatic with risible overtones, was hardly compelling, but in his treatment of it Hitchcock was able to invest a number of original touches. Some of these, such as adlibbed dialogue in one scene, and 'voice over' thoughts accompanied by a tight-lipped close-up, were to become screen clichés. Herbert Marshall played the thespian amateur detective in what according to Hitchcock was a send-up of one of the veteran theatrical figures of the day, Sir Gerald du Maurier. The beautiful victim of the processes of law, the girl languishing in the death cell, was played by Norah Baring.

The limitations of the sound medium at that date were such that in order to provide the background music when Herbert Marshall was giving voice to his inner thoughts with the radio playing in the background, a thirty-piece orchestra had to be physically present in the studio. In the jury room sequence impressionistic sound was used, and as the jurors reached their verdict they turned into a bizarre, chanting chorus. *Murder* was shot simultaneously in a German version, with a different cast, a practice common at the time. The language barrier proved insuperable, however, and the notably English elements, those concerned with social snobbery and behaviour, failed to come across. Hitchcock had convinced the German producers that the original script should not be changed, but when he came to shoot the film he realized, too late, that he was mistaken.

Social snobbery turned out to be the theme of his next film, an adaptation of John Galsworthy's play, *The Skin Game*. A drama of confrontation, it matched an upstart businessman against the traditional squirearchy, and with land as the valued prize showed the development of a vicious feud. Cynical and sardonic, the film seemed to have contempt for each side. Edmund Gwenn, hitherto a stage actor, was cast as the parvenu, performing with relish against the cold upper-class implacability of C. V. France and Helen Haye. Jack Cox was responsible for the photography, occasionally being permitted an outdoor shot of a sunlit wood to diminish the stage-ridden interiors. The most effective scene is a country auction where the two adversaries fiercely bid against each other. *The Skin Game*, an uncharacteristic Hitchcock film, could be said to be a study in the futility of snobbery.

It was followed by *Rich and Strange*, released in the early summer of 1932. The stars were Joan Barry, the actress who had dubbed the voice of Anny Ondra in *Blackmail* three years earlier, and Henry Kendall, an actor more familiar on the stage than the screen. They played a young married couple who, on inheriting some money, decide to leave their commuterland villa and embark on a world cruise. During the voyage their newly-acquired wealth affects their outlook and both fall for fortune hunters. The second part of the film is more serious in tone, with the chastened couple, now broke, making their way home, enduring en route a shipwreck and rescue by a Chinese junk. The return to England and the resumption of their former humdrum existence now does not seem so hard to bear.

Much of the film was shot on location in Marseilles, Port Said, Suez and Colombo without using sound. Only a fifth of the film does in fact have dialogue, in marked contrast to many of the films of the early talkie period where static cameras witnessed deluges of garrulousness. In common with much of Hitchcock's later work the story was allowed to develop visually. At one point a seasickness effect was created with the camera, having the result of conveying *mal de mer* to the unfortunate audience. Although Hitchcock personally liked the picture, there was little general enthusiasm when it first appeared; although his position as the leading British director was unchallenged, as much by default as anything else, it seemed that his career was running out of steam.

He then made his last film for B.I.P. at Elstree. Although *Number Seventeen* was a lightweight effort not to be taken too seriously, it was in the genre at which he excelled, the suspense thriller. It had been a play by Jefferson Farjeon, written for Leon M. Lion, who repeated his role of a tramp who discovers a jewel thieves' hideout in a sinister London house. A girl member of the gang falls in love with the detective investigating the case and saves his life. The rest of the film was a spectacular chase brilliantly using scale models of a

Above: Henry Kendall and Joan Barry at Waterloo ready to depart on the cruise that will change their lives in *Rich and Strange*

Below: Hitchcock at work on *Number Seventeen*, his last film for B.I.P.

Overleaf: Donald Calthrop and Garry Marsh on the footplate of a runaway locomotive in *Number Seventeen*

Inset: Jessie Matthews and Esmond Knight in *Waltzes from Vienna*, a film about the feud between Johann Strauss father and son

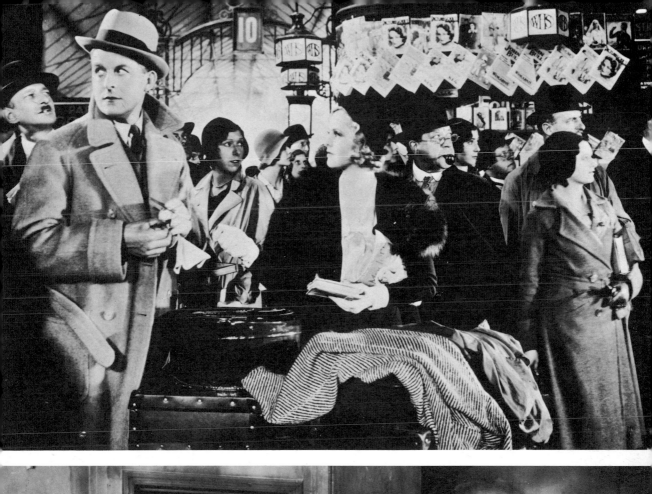

Green Line bus and a freight train which were pitted against each other in a frantic dash to the coast. The climax showed the train rushing out of control on to the train ferry in its berth at Dover at full speed, roaring through the ship and into the sea beyond. The chase sequence was shot with great verve, the crooks leaping from one wagon to another against the night sky, and rapid cross-cutting between the commandeered bus and the train providing breathtaking visual suspense. The plot was riddled with absurdities – a man calling at the house well after midnight announcing that an estate agent had sent him to look over the place, the mute girl member of the gang bursting into speech with: 'I'm not really dumb. It was just a crook's trick' without explaining the purpose. It was a short film, little more than an hour in length, and shot on a low budget. Hitchcock could make much of thin material.

In his last year at Elstree he worked as production supervisor as well as director, and in the closing months there he produced the only film which he did not direct himself, *Lord Camber's Ladies*, a low-budget work starring Gertrude Lawrence, and directed by Benn W. Levy, who had written much of the dialogue of *Blackmail*. It was a so-called 'quota quickie' made to satisfy the requirements of screen time in British cinemas devoted to a British product. It was of little consequence.

Hitchcock left the studio and went to Shepherd's Bush to make a film for Tom Arnold. It fell so far outside the Hitchcock canon that it was not surprising that it was regarded as an unqualified disaster. *Waltzes from Vienna* concerned a musical feud between Johann Strauss senior and junior. In spite of a cast that included Jessie Matthews, Fay Compton, Edmund Gwenn, Esmond Knight and Frank Vosper, its production values were low; a musical, according to Hitchcock, where they really couldn't afford the music. Esmond Knight, writing in his autobiography, said: 'When *Waltzes from Vienna* was only half-finished Hitch had tired of it and, I think, had begun to realize that he had made a mistake, and after an exhausting day in a stuffy studio in which an enormous crowd of extras were assembled he announced, "I hate this sort of stuff. Melodrama is the only thing I can do!"'

Although at this time he was at a low ebb in his career he was approached by Michael Balcon, who had set him on the directorial path nearly ten years before. As has been said before, Balcon's extraordinary prescience was to lead to the discovery and encouragement of several major British film directors, but none more outstanding than Alfred Hitchcock. And it was at this time, at Balcon's instigation, that he was to embark upon the magnificent series of thrillers that were to comprise what is usually referred to as his Gaumont-British period, although that company was to go out of production later in the thirties, the last film being made under the Gainsborough banner.

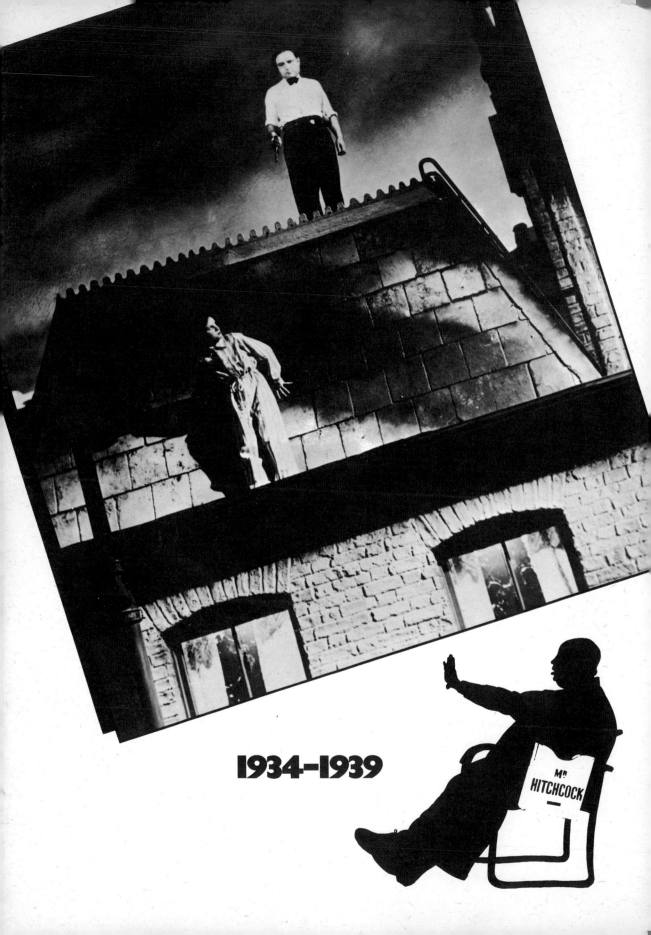

1934-1939

The first of the films had already been written while Hitchcock was at work on the wretched *Waltzes from Vienna*. The thought that he had the screenplay of *The Man Who Knew Too Much* in his back pocket was one of the few things that sustained him during that unhappy production. It was a source of amusement to Hitchcock that when the later film was released it was hailed as a masterly comeback for a director who had gone into decline. Said Hitchcock: 'The irony was that it was made, in my mind anyway, before *Waltzes from Vienna*.' *The Man Who Knew Too Much* was the only film that Hitchcock was to remake completely, although in several other films he was to return to similar themes. There were few differences between the 1934 and the 1956 versions of *The Man Who Knew Too Much*, probably the most striking being the relocation of the opening sequence from the ski slopes of Switzerland to the market place of Marrakesh. The 1934 film opened with the assassination of a secret agent at St Moritz. The agent, before expiring, manages to pass on information concerning the forthcoming attempt on the life of a foreign diplomat visiting London to an English couple who are holidaying at the resort. Before they can in turn tell the authorities, the plotters kidnap their little daughter, thus ensuring their silence. The climax of the film takes place at the Royal Albert Hall during a concert attended by the distinguished visitor, and the assassination attempt is foiled by the wife screaming from the audience at the crucial moment, putting the sniper off his aim. This sequence is followed by a gun battle between the police and the spies in their East End hideout, with very obvious similarities in its staging to the famous Sidney Street siege of twenty-five years earlier. The chief villain was played by Peter Lorre in his first British film. After his success in Fritz Lang's *M* he had left Germany as the Nazis came to power. Leslie Banks and Edna Best played the distraught parents and a youthful Nova Pilbeam played the young girl.

The pace of the film was vigorous and the exposition of the plot was larded with red herrings to keep the audience guessing. The concert scene was brilliantly filmed, with the suspense mounting second by second as a cantata moves towards a peak when the cymbals are clashed. This was the moment to cue the assassin; the crack of his rifle being drowned by the music. The unlikely source of this idea had been a cartoon sequence in *Punch* by H. M. Bateman, in which a little man gets up, goes through the routine of washing, dressing and journeying to a concert where he sits waiting to play his one note before returning home, going through the reverse procedure to get back into bed. Considerable economy was effected in shooting the Albert Hall scenes, with much use of the Schufftan process, whereby most of the audience was merely a glass-painted reflection. The artist engaged to depict the audience was the academician Fortunino Mantania. Hitchcock in

In *The Man Who Knew Too Much* kidnapped child Nova Pilbeam is threatened by a spy when she makes an escape attempt. Below rages a street battle between police and anarchists

retrospect prefers the 1956 version, however, feeling that the first film was untidy structurally.

His next film was another exciting foray into the world of spies and secret plots, using as its basis one of the classic adventure stories by a master narrator, and discarding virtually everything in the book but for the name of the hero, Richard Hannay. Yet *The Thirty Nine Steps*, the screen version of which originally gave its imperialist originator John Buchan severe alarm, turned out to be one of the most successful films of 1935, and eventually earned grudging praise from its creator. Certainly it would be fair to say that much of the spirit of Buchan's yarn had been kept, but that the Hitchcock version was far more fun. Robert Donat played the young colonial hero, enjoying a visit from Canada to the old country, and almost at once becoming involved in a spy intrigue. A mysterious woman insists that he shelters her in his rented apartment as there are men out to murder her. Only half-believing her story he lets her stay in his living room, but is awoken when she staggers into his bedroom with a knife in her back. She warns him to flee before dropping dead across his bed. He escapes from London with the press and police after him. They are under the impression that he is the killer. After an arduous journey to Scotland he stumbles on the lair of the master spy, outwardly a figure of considerable respectability in his neighbourhood. A girl he met on the train and who has attempted to hand him over to the police is somehow handcuffed to him and together they make a strained dash across the moors. She is only convinced of his innocence after a night at a country inn. At the end of the film all is revealed from the stage of the London Palladium, where a memory man is shown to be unwillingly passing on secrets to a foreign power.

The screenplay was by Charles Bennett and Ian Hay, with
Hitchcock, as was his custom, playing a large part in the con-
struction of the story. Many elements that were not present in
the Buchan original were incorporated, the most important
being the romantic interest, with Madeleine Carroll playing
with great success another of the ice-cool blondes – at first
antipathetic towards the hero, but later acquiescent. She
joined the gallery in which Anny Ondra, Ingrid Bergman,
Joan Fontaine, Kim Novak, Grace Kelly, Eva Marie Saint and
Tippi Hedren all had places.

Hannay was played by Robert Donat, a pleasant young
romantic actor whose career was already blighted by asthma
which somehow gave strength to his reedy, thin voice. The
film was a double chase in the best Hitchcockian tradition, the
hero on the run from both the police and the villains. Each
episode flowed naturally into the next, providing for the audience a relentless pace and excitement, even if the rapidity at
which the plot moved disguised flaws in its logical progression
that would not have been tolerated in a more measured film.
One of the biggest concerned the nature of the thirty-nine
steps themselves. In Buchan's novel they are the number of
steps leading down the cliffs near Dover to the spies' secret
landing-place, but since no such scene existed in the film they
became merely the obscure and unexplained name of the spy
organization, blurted out in the final sequence by the unfortunate Mr Memory before he succumbed to a fatal bullet wound.
It is an oft-quoted theory of Hitchcock's that providing the
action is keeping the audience interested they will care little
for the exact nature of the menace, secret plots and plans and
all the other paraphernalia of intrigue – it is enough that they
are causing the people on the screen to go frantic. He calls

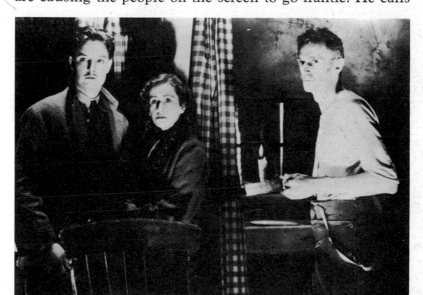

the device the 'MacGuffin' and his films abound with them.

Another Hitchcockian touch very evident in *The Thirty
Nine Steps* is the intrusion into the fabric of ordinary, everyday
life of the highly-charged world of spies and master criminals,
gratuitous violence and sudden death. Thus when the arch
villain is about to gun down the hero the drawing room setting
is established by the entrance of his wife, the unruffled grande
dame Helen Haye, to announce that lunch is ready. There is
the brief, but effective scene in which Hannay takes refuge in a
crofter's cottage. The crofter is dour and proud as only John
Laurie could play him, but his wife (Peggy Ashcroft) is timid,
withdrawn and frightened. She is perceptive enough to realize
that the visitor is a wanted man and by eye gestures is able to
convey that she will help. The husband, half aware of what is
happening suspects a romantic understanding, and finds an
excuse to go outside so that he can peer through the window,
as though deliberately inciting his wife to be unfaithful.

There is frequently a strong thread of sexual violence in
Hitchcock's films; an example in *The Thirty Nine Steps*
comes to mind in which the man and the woman find themselves handcuffed together. There is something curious, too,
in the conversation of the two middle-aged sales representa-
tives on the train, which turns on the nature of the wares they
are peddling: repulsive-looking rubber foundation garments
with large, pendulous suspenders.

Hitchcock shoots the
famous handcuff sequence
in *The Thirty Nine Steps*.
Chained together, Robert
Donat and Madeleine
Carroll scramble across the
studio rocks and heather
in search of a friendly inn

The film was a considerable success both in Britain and the United States, where Hitchcock was one of the few British film directors to have a commonly recognized name. He was receiving and turning down offers to film in Hollywood, and, fortunately for the film industry, was to continue working in Britain until the end of the decade.

Charles Bennett worked on the screenplay of the next film, which was adapted from a play by Campbell Dixon, in turn based on Somerset Maugham's Ashenden. It was called *The Secret Agent* and John Gielgud was cast as the successful novelist inducted into the secret service on account of the exigencies of wartime; Madeleine Carroll played his bogus wife. They are both novices in the game. On a mission to Switzerland he kills an innocent man in the belief that he is a spy and as a consequence undergoes agonies of guilt, shrugged off by his companion, a genial Mexican murderer played by Peter Lorre. Eventually they locate the real spy, a suave American played by Robert Young. A train on which the principal parties are all travelling is bombed and crashes spectacularly. The Mexican is shot by the spy before he himself dies. Ashenden returns to England, chastened and resolved never to get mixed up in espionage again.

As in the preceding film there were many rich Hitchcockian touches – a Swiss chocolate factory being the cover for the spy

John Gielgud and Madeleine Carroll survive a train wreck in *The Secret Agent*, while Peter Lorre calmly takes liquid sustenance

bureau, for instance. A single sustained organ note ringing out across a valley is discovered within the church to be caused by a body slumped across the keyboard. The powerful element of guilt that motivates the Gielgud character is an echo of that which forced Hannay to avenge the murder of a woman who came to him for protection. The adversary in *The Secret Agent* was as attractive a person as the hero – charming, cultivated, witty – and is an example of the way in which Hitchcock likes to invert stereotypes. But the film was less of a success than *The Thirty Nine Steps*, and Hitchcock has ascribed its relative failure to the negative characterization of the Gielgud role. 'You can't root for a hero who doesn't want to be a hero,' is how he sums it up.

It was the second of four Hitchcock films to be photographed by Bernard Knowles, who had also shot *The Thirty Nine Steps*. He was later to become a director in his own right, making his debut with a romantic ghost story not without Hitchcockian overtones, *A Place of One's Own* (1945), but his subsequent work failed to live up to its promise.

The Hitchcock film following *The Secret Agent* was a film version of a novel by Joseph Conrad, also called *The Secret Agent* and retitled by Hitchcock for film purposes *Sabotage*. Confusion was compounded a few years later when he made a film called *Saboteur*. In any case, *Sabotage* was known as *A Woman Alone* in America. The screenplay was again by

Madeleine Carroll, John Gielgud and Hitchcock on the set of *The Secret Agent*

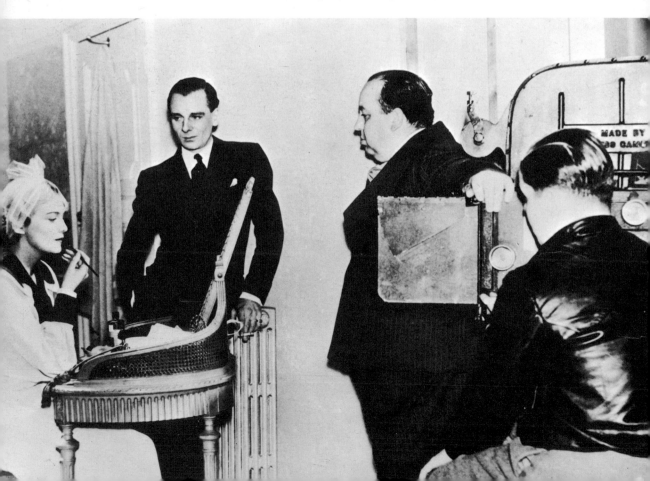

Charles Bennett, and the editor was Charles Frend, who was to become a notable Ealing director, responsible for such pictures as *The Foreman Went to France* and *The Cruel Sea*.

Oscar Homolka played a London anarchist, whose cover was the proprietorship of a small local cinema. His unknowing wife was played by the American actress Sylvia Sidney, and a suspicious detective, disguised as a neighbouring shop assistant, by John Loder. The climactic sequence of the film followed the journey of the wife's young brother across London, unaware that the film containers he is carrying conceal a bomb timed to destroy Piccadilly Circus underground station. Unfortunately the boy procrastinates so much during the journey, which is also interrupted by the Lord Mayor's Show, that he and the bus in which he is riding are blown to smithereens on the appointed hour. It is, Hitchcock admits, a fatal mistake in a film to build up the suspense and sympathy for an innocent person on the screen, and then let him be killed. It's as though the girl tied to the railway tracks is really run over by the train, with no sign of a last minute rescue.

As a result of the death of her brother the wife reaches a decision to kill her husband while he is eating his evening meal. There is no dialogue in the scene – she is carving the meat and looks down at the knife realizing that it could be a weapon. Her husband sees her and realizes the same thing. He gets up and crosses the table to face her. She pushes the knife

Oscar Homolka and Sylvia Sidney in *Sabotage*. Homolka played the leader of a group of anarchist plotters in London, and Sylvia Sidney his unsuspecting wife

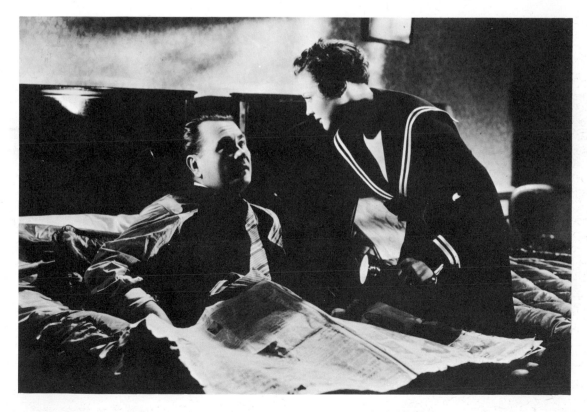

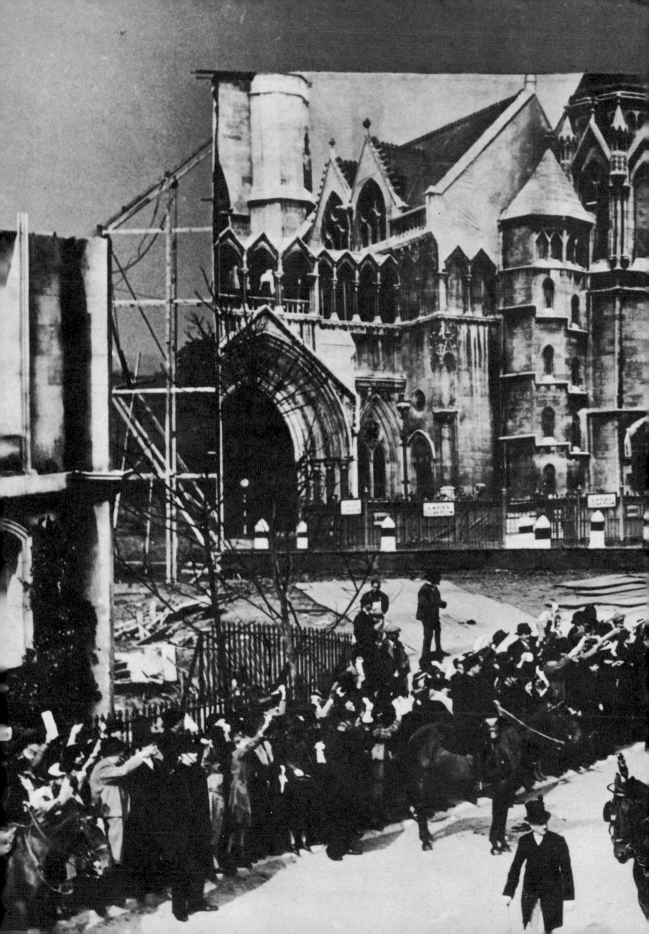

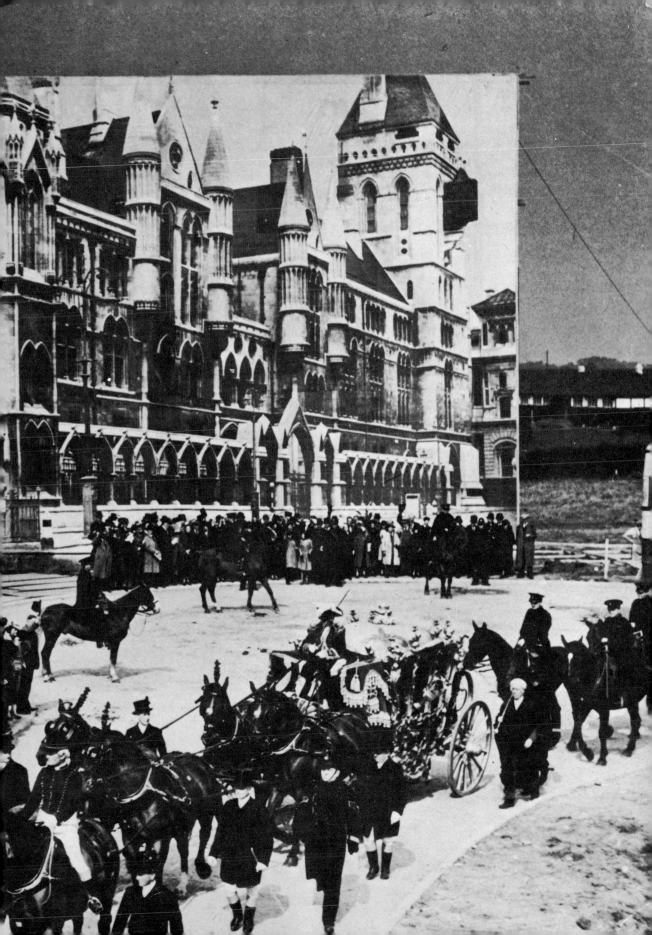

into his stomach. It is as though, begging for remorse, he has willed her to kill him. At the film's end a fortuitous explosion destroys the evidence of her crime.

Hitchcock was disappointed with the casting of the detective. He had wanted Robert Donat for the part, but Alexander Korda was unwilling to release him from his contract. It meant that much of John Loder's dialogue had been rewritten, but even so he was still unsuitable. Oscar Homolka, ostensibly the villain of the piece, came out far more sympathetically.

Sabotage was the last Hitchcock film to be produced by Michael Balcon, who then left Gaumont-British to take charge of production at the newly-formed MGM British company, but after making *A Yank at Oxford* for them he had a disagreement with Louis B. Mayer and went into independent production at Ealing.

In 1937 Gaumont-British, plunging deep into financial crisis, abandoned film production, but retained their distribution interests. Lime Grove Studios at Shepherd's Bush stayed in the film business under the aegis of Gainsborough Pictures, who also continued production at their Islington Studios. Hitchcock made *Young and Innocent* for them, both at Lime Grove and at the newly-opened Pinewood Studios which were able to offer a sound stage big enough for one of the most spectacular shots of his career, a crane tracking in from a distance of 145 feet across a crowded ballroom, to within four inches of the twitching eye of a black-faced drummer. *Young and Innocent* (*The Girl Was Young* in America) was another double chase picture, with the young hero (Derrick de Marney) wrongly suspected of murdering a girl. He escapes from a courthouse and seeks help from a girl (Nova Pilbeam) not realizing that she is the daughter of the chief constable. She overcomes her initial antagonism towards him, and convinced of his innocence, helps him to find the actual murderer. The screenplay was again by Charles Bennett, adapted from a novel called *A Shilling for Candles* by Josephine Tey. It marked the end of Bennett's association with Hitchcock on British films, for he left to go to America on contract with David O. Selznick.

The settings of *Young and Innocent* were fresh and pleasant, the opening sequence being shot on location in a summery Cornwall. It was a comedy thriller with a light touch – a typical scene being the arrival of the fugitive couple at a grotesque children's party staged by the girl's aunt, with the hero attempting to establish his bona fides by offering a birthday present which is in reality a garden ornament hastily appropriated on his way into the house. It is Hitchcock's favourite among his British films.

The next was also made for Gainsborough with the same producer, Edward Black. *The Lady Vanishes* was scripted by Frank Launder and Sidney Gilliatt from a novel called *The Wheel Spins* by Ethel Lina White. Jack Cox returned to Hitch-

Above: Hitchcock's token appearance in *Young and Innocent* was as an onlooker with a box camera outside the doors of the courthouse

Below: A remarkable crane shot in *Young and Innocent*, in which the camera tracks 145 feet across a crowded dance floor to within four inches of the twitching eye of the drummer

Overleaf: Michael Redgrave, Margaret Lockwood and Dame May Whitty in *The Lady Vanishes*, about an English governess who disappears on a train hurtling through a Central European country

Inset: Margaret Lockwood with Hitchcock on the set of *The Lady Vanishes*

MR HITCHCOCK

cock to photograph it. A distribution deal with MGM enabled a wider audience to see the film, and its arrival in London during the period of the Munich crisis in the autumn of 1938 was a useful ill wind in ensuring its success, for its topicality with strange goings-on in middle Europe attracted the public.

It was a return to spies and intrigue. A young, rather self-confident girl (a brunette this time, Margaret Lockwood) while on a Balkan holiday becomes friendly with an English governess. During a train journey the middle-aged woman vanishes and attempts are made to convince the girl that she never really existed. She enlists the aid of a donnish young man (Michael Redgrave making his film debut) who is a composer and collector of folksongs and who had previously been irritating her. They learn that the woman is a British secret agent trying to return to England with vital information and that she has been kidnapped on the train by the foreign power in whose territory they are travelling. Eventually the train is shunted on to a branch line where it is the centre of a pitched battle between the British passengers and the secret state police. On reaching England the couple are greeted by the woman they saved, and she plays the folk song in which the vital message is concealed. Basil Radford and Naunton Wayne made their film debut in their celebrated double act as a pair of fat-headed, cricket-obsessed Englishmen, anxious to return home only in order to catch the remaining hours of a test match, which turned out to be rained off anyway.

Thematically *The Lady Vanishes* is very much a Hitchcock movie. The setting of the main part of the action on a train is a favourite device. The speed of the plot is so breathtaking that the implausibilities are glossed over. If one stops to ask why the British government is relying on little old ladies to bring home their essential foreign information or why it should be concealed in the melody of a Balkan folksong, one is lost. This is the Hitchcock MacGuffin in action. Redgrave and Lockwood maintain a typically bickering relationship during the first part of the film, and the thaw does not set in until the mystery has really deepened. Vital evidence of the woman's existence hangs fleetingly before the eyes of heroine and audience in the form of a label from her special tea packet adhering to the train window, but then whisks away before anyone else can see it. The giveaway eventually comes with the unlikely clue of a bogus nun wearing high heels, a mistake that the conspirators, with all the care that had gone into their subterfuge, would hardly have been likely to have made.

Launder and Gilliatt went on to establish a successful production team of their own, producing two or three thrillers in a Hitchcockian vein, such as *I See a Dark Stranger* and *Green for Danger* before succumbing to that regrettable tendency of so many British film-makers to concentrate on broad comedy, such as the St Trinian's series. Margaret Lockwood was to

Left: Hitchcock in story
conference with Erich
Pommer (on Hitchcock's
right) for *Jamaica Inn*.
Their leading actor is
Charles Laughton (on
Pommer's right in hat)

Below left: Marie Ney,
Leslie Banks and Maureen
O'Hara in *Jamaica Inn*

Below right: Charles
Laughton as the villainous
magistrate and Robert
Newton as his adversary

enjoy a position of eminence at the top of the list of box-office stars in the forties. *The Lady Vanishes* was the last of six excellent thrillers Hitchcock made in England in the thirties.

In 1937 at the invitation of David O. Selznick he had gone to the United States for the first time. He decided to accept an offer to work for Selznick in Hollywood, but as the contract did not become operative until the spring of 1939 he prepared to make one last film in England. It was an unfortunate choice though it brought a return to Elstree and a renewed association with Erich Pommer, who had produced his first film and was to produce this one in company with Charles Laughton, who was to play a leading part as well. It was *Jamaica Inn*, from a novel by Daphne du Maurier. The script was by Sidney Gilliatt and Joan Harrison, with J. B. Priestley drafted in to write special dialogue for Laughton. A costume melodrama, it was concerned with the discovery by an Irish girl staying with her aunt at a remote Cornish inn that the place was a base for a band of smugglers and wreckers. She appeals to the local squire and magistrate, not realizing that he is the ringleader. He kidnaps her, but is shot dead by a member of the ship's crew who has succumbed to the heroine's Irish charm. Maureen O'Hara made what she could with the bland role of the girl, and Emyln Williams was a memorable wrecker. But the film was grotesquely overshadowed by the extravagant performance of Charles Laughton as Sir Humphrey Penhaligon, the wicked squire. It was obvious that he was beyond the control of the director, and Hitchcock was wont in such circumstances to shrug, and look forward to making his next film. *Jamaica Inn* was undistinguished and structurally creaky. Even with Laughton's spectacular demise, plunging headlong from the rigging of his ship to the deck below (falls from a great height are a fairly common way for Hitchcockian heavies to meet their doom) there is a marked lack of enthusiasm in all this early 19th century nonsense, and costume pictures have never been his forte. It was sad that his British career should have ended on a low note, even though the film was well-received at the box office. This was an indication of the esteem in which he was held by the general public, as well as the drawing power of the cast, including the egregious Laughton, whose bravura acting was unaccountably vogueish in the thirties.

In the summer of 1939 Hitchcock sold his two homes – in London and Shamley Green, Surrey– and with his wife, daughter and Joan Harrison, his assistant, set sail for America, a country of which he had a profound knowledge from boyhood. His move across the Atlantic was inevitable since he had always recognized that the prime, most professional fountainhead of the English-speaking cinema lay not in Britain, but in Hollywood, and his apprenticeship and training in films had been with American companies. The only wonder was that it took him so long to get there, for by now he was forty.

47

1940-1943

Although he had signed with Selznick initially to direct a story about the sinking of the *Titanic*, by the time he reached Hollywood it had been decided that his first film there would be from another best-selling Daphne du Maurier novel, *Rebecca*. The *Titanic* film was never made.

Set in Cornwall again, *Rebecca* was concerned with the overwhelming memory of a landowner's dead wife, which was blighting his second marriage. As the story developed the man was suspected of murdering Rebecca, the dead woman, whose unseen presence seemed to permeate the stonework of Manderley, the vast mansion that was the family home. An obsessive housekeeper is striving bitterly to keep Rebecca's spirit active while destroying the second wife by emphasizing her discomfort and gaucherie. Eventually the mystery of Rebecca's death by drowning is solved and the housekeeper kills herself, after firing the great house. A melodramatic plot perhaps, but Hitchcock presented the action with a polish and technical excellence now made possible by the superior resources available to him in American studios.

An impressive, mainly British cast was headed by Laurence Olivier as Maxim de Winter, the master of Manderley, Joan Fontaine as his bride, Judith Anderson as the sinister housekeeper and George Sanders as a shifty friend. The Englishness of the cast list was continued with such performers as C. Aubrey Smith, Reginald Denny, Nigel Bruce, Leo G. Carroll and Gladys Cooper in supporting roles. Hitchcock has speculated on what would have happened if the film had been shot in England, and concludes that it would have lost much of its dreamlike, magical quality.

The musical score by Franz Waxman provided a haunting, melodic theme which heightened the mystery, especially when accompanied by beautiful tracking shots of the corridors and staircases of the old mansion. Judith Anderson's aura of menace was conveyed by Hitchcock's avoidance of shots showing her entering a room. Joan Fontaine would turn, and there she would be as though materialized through the floor, subtly evoking a feeling of creepy unpredictability. Joan Fontaine had to work hard to suggest her unease at finding herself mistress of such a grand house – her dinner-table clumsiness and failure to exert herself over the servants culminate in the painful gaffe on the night of a fancy-dress ball when she appears in a dress identical to that worn by the first Mrs de Winter.

Rebecca was an outstanding box-office success throughout the world, and was exceptionally well-reviewed by the American critics. It won the Academy Award as the best film of 1940, the only Hitchcock film to be so honoured.

In Europe the war had gathered momentum and Hitchcock, being over military age, was advised by the British government to stay where he was. Early in 1940 he became involved in making a film for Walter Wanger. It was *Foreign*

Robert Cummings and Priscilla Lane in *Saboteur*. The chase theme of *The Thirty Nine Steps* was transposed to wartime America, with Cummings as a young factory worker wrongly accused of burning his airplane plant

Above: Hitchcock in Hollywood, shooting Laurence Olivier and Joan Fontaine in a scene from *Rebecca*, Hitchcock's first American film

Left: Joan Fontaine and Laurence Olivier in the same film

Above right: Diane Baker, Tippi Hedren and Alan Napier in *Marnie*

Right: Sean Connery and Tippi Hedren in the same film

Correspondent, a spy thriller with propaganda overtones. Joel McCrea played a crime reporter switched by his cynical American newspaper proprietor to cover the European scene where war is impending – a subject he knows nothing about. He meets a Dutch statesman who is attempting to get a secret peace treaty back to his government, but is kidnapped by the Nazis. He falls in love with the daughter of a pacifist leader (Herbert Marshall) who is in reality the head of a Nazi spy ring. At the outbreak of war the main players are en route for neutral America aboard a clipper flying boat, but the plane is shot down. The master spy dies heroically while saving the life of his daughter. The reporter returns to London and as the bombs begin to fall is broadcasting the grim warning to America to remember the plight of Europe.

Hitchcock was disappointed in the casting of McCrea in the leading role and would have preferred Gary Cooper, or Cary Grant who is now known to have turned down the script. Laraine Day as the girl was also an actress in the second league. But in the impeccable Herbert Marshall Hitchcock had an excellent villain, a refined upper-class Englishman of cultivated charm and ultimately great courage. Edmund Gwenn also occupied a small but telling part as an engaging little assassin whose *modus operandi* was to lure his victim to the top of a tall building from which he could push him off. One of the most effective scenes was the assassination of a statesman in Amsterdam in pouring rain. The killer, posing as a press photographer, had a gun concealed in his camera and made his escape through the crowd, seen as a sea of bobbing umbrellas. McCrea, having given chase out of the city into the open countryside, is bemused by the sails of one windmill turning in a direction contrary to all the others. It is very appropriately the rallying point for the spy network and a signal for a landing aircraft.

The penultimate sequence in which the flying boat is shot down in mid-Atlantic represented an ingenious use of the studio tank. The headlong rush towards the water is shown from inside the cabin; as the plane hits the surface the control deck is rent asunder by a cascade of water, drowning the pilots. It was shot in one take, no cuts, using a transparent screen, front projection and a concealed water tank ruptured at the right moment.

It is said that *Foreign Correspondent* evinced great interest with Dr Goebbels, the Nazi head of propaganda. It was certainly popular with audiences, and with *Rebecca* was on the list of the ten best films of 1940 in the *Motion Picture Herald*. Its appearance in England at the commencement of the London blitz brought a prophetic note to its last scene, and in America it would have been seen as an attack on the prevailing policy of isolationism only lately breached by Roosevelt's lend-lease, and a warning of the methods of the so-called fifth

Tippi Hedren under attack in *The Birds*

Left: Assassination in
Amsterdam—a dramatic
scene from *Foreign
Correspondent*

Above: Hitchcock makes
his fleeting appearance

Below: Albert Basserman
as a kidnapped prisoner

column. It was over a year before Pearl Harbor. The style and pace of the film was in marked contrast to the sedate *Rebecca*.

The next film was also a drastic change of step. *Mr and Mrs Smith*, made by Hitchcock at RKO in 1941, was the first of his Hollywood films to have an all-American setting. A marital comedy, it was based on a screenplay by Norman Krasna which Hitchcock apparently inherited and filmed more or less as it stood. It is a routine and unremarkable picture, without any very noticeable Hitchcock signatures, and might have been disastrous were it not for the casting of the magnificent and beautiful comedy actress Carole Lombard as the leading lady. She was teamed with Robert Montgomery, playing her husband, a New York lawyer, who discovers that by some technicality their marriage, accomplished years earlier, is void. He is forced to court his wife anew in the teeth of fierce competition from a rival played by Gene Raymond. In a small part was Betty Compson, who had been the expensive star of *Woman to Woman*, the first film on which Hitchcock had been assistant director in the twenties. On the first day of shooting of *Mr and Mrs Smith* Carole Lombard organized a practical joke at Hitchcock's expense, taking as her inspiration his oft-quoted remark that actors were cattle. On the sound stage she had a small corral installed, stocking it with calves bearing labels with the names of the leading players.

Jack Carson, Carole Lombard and Robert Montgomery in *Mr and Mrs Smith*. The genre of sophisticated comedy was unusual for Hitchcock

The next film was also made for RKO, and for *Suspicion* Hitchcock was at last able to secure the services of Cary Grant, who was to become one of his most-favoured actors. Grant shared the distinction with James Stewart of starring in no less than four Hitchcock films, and *Suspicion* was the first. He was teamed opposite Joan Fontaine, who somewhat surprisingly won the best actress of 1941 Oscar for her performance.

Like *Rebecca*, the film was set in England, with Joan Fontaine as a well-bred but shy girl, who becomes infatuated and marries Cary Grant, a shiftless, apparently impractical spendthrift. Following the death of one of his odd friends she suspects that he is a murderer and after her fortune, and works herself into a state of nervous illness as she imagines his every move being directed towards her destruction. At the last minute her fears are proved to be groundless. This was an ending which went against the grain as far as Hitchcock was concerned, but was forced upon him by the studio front office fearful that Cary Grant's box-office stature would be diminished were he to be made a villain.

The story was originally a book called *Before the Fact* by Francis Iles, and the screenplay was by Samson Raphaelson, with assistance from Joan Harrison and Alma Reville. In spite of the amendment of the original plot a studio executive felt that there were still too many indications that Grant was really

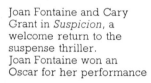

Joan Fontaine and Cary Grant in *Suspicion*, a welcome return to the suspense thriller.
Joan Fontaine won an Oscar for her performance

a murderer, and in Hitchcock's absence he ordered them to be deleted, which meant that the film was trimmed to a mere fifty-five minutes, a ludicrous playing time. Fortunately, after a battle the footage was restored and the film was released. It is not an entirely satisfying work, the teasing of the audience being rather more prominent than is usual and it is plain that Hitchcock's enthusiasm for the situation waned at some stage. But it is sumptuously set in the England that only Hollywood can create, a Mrs Miniver-land of palatial mansions and landed gentry.

Saboteur was made after Pearl Harbor and the American entry into the war. A munitions worker, played by Robert Cummings, is wrongly accused of sabotage, after his plant has burned down. It is *The Thirty Nine Steps* and *Young and Innocent* in an American wartime setting. He escapes from the authorities and sets out on a cross-country marathon in search of the real culprits. As in *The Thirty Nine Steps* he has at one point to conceal the fact that he has been handcuffed, and to convince a sceptical girl that he is not a fugitive lawbreaker. The chase leads across America via such locations as the Boulder Dam and a desert ghost town with a denouement on the torch of the Statue of Liberty. There the trapped Nazi agent literally dangles by his coat threads until all have parted, causing him to plunge hundreds of feet to his death; the hero is left holding an empty sleeve. There is another echo of *The Thirty Nine Steps*, and for that matter *Jamaica Inn* and *Foreign Correspondent*, in that the master villain is on the surface a respected member of the community.

Hitchcock had wanted Harry Carey to take the part in order to play up the patriotic American disguise, but the wife of the veteran Western star objected to him portraying an America Firster (a neo-Nazi), with the result that the part went to Otto Kruger who played it in a less subtle manner, as a conventional sinister heavy. Poor casting blighted the film, for Hitchcock would rather have used Gary Cooper and Barbara Stanwyck, neither of whom ever played in one of his films, for the parts taken by Robert Cummings, a pleasant but lightweight actor, and Priscilla Lane, a routine actress, not a major star. Instinctively, Hitchcock felt that audiences were less likely to respond to a hero's predicament if he was not played by a big star. There was, consequently, a certain flatness about the film, in spite of the excitement and pace of the narrative.

The story was an original by Hitchcock himself, for which the producers, Frank Lloyd and Jack Skirball, paid $70,000 on condition that he directed it himself. Some of the dialogue was written by Dorothy Parker, who had much fun in a sequence in which the couple were assisted in their flight by a troupe of circus freaks. Norman Lloyd, apart from falling horribly from the Statue of Liberty, performed so well as the real saboteur that he suffered later from the typecasting syndrome. A neat

Above: Priscilla Lane, Alan Baxter and Robert Cummings in *Saboteur*

topical touch was included; as he rides in a car along the New York waterfront and looks out at the capsized hull of the French liner *Normandie*, which turned over and burned early in the war, he smirks, clearly implying that it was the work of his fellow saboteurs – an implication much resented at the time by the U.S. Navy, as there was no proof that the sinking had been sabotage. It could be said that *North by Northwest*, made years later, was a remake of *Saboteur*, but with a tighter discipline of the material and with a stronger star in the lead.

In 1943 Hitchcock made *Shadow of a Doubt*, one of the best of his American films, and one that he himself cherishes. It was shot mainly on location in a small northern Californian town called Santa Rosa, using the streets, buildings and people of the community as background, and so avoiding the studio look of so many of the films of the forties. The screenplay was worked out in collaboration with the playwright Thornton Wilder, who as author of *Our Town* had a vested interest in the grassroots of smalltown America. The central figure was a debonair, fastidious Easterner – a murderer of wealthy widows, who moves west to hide out at the home of his unknowing sister. His pretty niece, known like him as Charlie, has an instant rapport with him, but at the same time suspects that something is wrong. She discovers his appalling secret and he, realizing that the jig is nearly up, makes attempts on her life. In the final one he himself is killed by the train he tries to push her under, and with the agreement of a detective who has followed out from the east, he is allowed a normal funeral; the crimes are withheld from the grieving family.

Joseph Cotten played Uncle Charlie with panache and Teresa Wright was excellently cast as the niece. Each counterpointed the other, good and evil locked in combat. Yet the audience was made to feel great sympathy for the murderer, and to some extent shared the girl's regard for him, yet knowing as she did that she must destroy him.

There was an interesting device used to identify the Uncle Charlie murders, known as the Merry Widow killings. An insert of swirling couples was used with 'The Merry Widow' waltz playing on the soundtrack, both in the credits and at other points in the film. During a discussion at the dinner table when everyone is attempting to identify the tune, Charlie glibly says that it is 'The Blue Danube', but his niece is aware that he is faking. Overlapping conversations, a technique used by Orson Welles in *Citizen Kane*, are used to good effect, helping the dialogue to sound unprepared and real. Undoubtedly much of the appeal of the film lay in the careful evocation of the everyday atmosphere of smalltown life, and the techniques were some way ahead of their time, so much so that the film's freshness is still apparent more than thirty years later. The only weak casting was MacDonald Carey as the young detective, who is also meant to supply a romantic interest.

Below: Joseph Cotten as the murderer in *Shadow of a Doubt*, in which a psychopathic killer hides out with unsuspecting relations

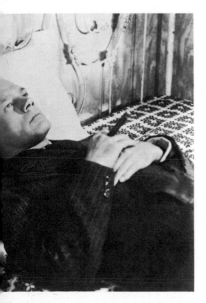

With *Lifeboat* Hitchcock set himself one of his most formidable challenges. The action of the film was confined to a lifeboat bobbing up and down in the Atlantic, bearing the survivors of a torpedoed passenger ship and the U-boat commander of the submarine that sank it. Thus the world conflict was distilled into a mid-ocean confrontation on a tiny boat. The whole film was shot in the studio tank at Twentieth-Century Fox. Each of the survivors represented a stereotype: John Hodiak as a left-wing stoker, Henry Hull as a business tycoon, Canada Lee as a negro steward, Tallulah Bankhead as a sophisticated New York journalist and Walter Slezak as a resourceful, self-contained Nazi.

The occupants debate whether the Nazi should even be allowed aboard, but when it is clear that his knowledge of seamanship is superior to everyone else's they let him take control of the navigation. Later they learn that he has been stealing extra rations for himself, and is steering them not to safety but towards a German supply ship. A wounded sailor who alone realized what was happening was thrown overboard. Aroused by the beast, the other occupants of the boat, normal, civilized people when they entered it, now rise up and meet ruthlessness with ruthlessness, beating the Nazi to death like an animal pack. The film demonstrates, therefore, the effect of war on human attitudes – all the characters undergo shifts in their outlook, although none more drastic than that of the woman journalist. She starts out regarding the whole thing as another 'scoop' – a true adventure with which to earn kudos back at base – but as she loses her possessions, first her camera, then her typewriter, and later a valuable and sentimentally precious bracelet, she changes from arrogant cynic to concerned crew member; barriers are stripped away.

The critics of the day fell upon the film for the portrayal of the Nazi. In the middle of the war they found it hard to accept that a member of the master race could be shown as the most powerful and knowledgeable figure in the boat, the one with the strongest will for survival and the capacity to bring it about. On modern viewing such criticism seems curious; the U-boat captain is still portrayed as a conventional Nazi heavy, bent on treachery and murder, with not a shred of humanity anywhere in his make-up. In many war films Germans were depicted as heel-clicking, unimaginative, sadistic dunderheads, but Hitchcock was insisting the enemy should not be underestimated.

A minor dilemma confronted Hitchcock in finding an opportunity to make his customary personal appearance. With the claustrophobic setting and a cast of only nine actors he could scarcely intrude. The problem was solved by allowing William Bendix to pick up and read an old newspaper. An advertisement on the back was in the form of a 'before' and 'after' pitch for a mythical product, a slimming drug called Reduco, and the model for the pictures was Alfred Hitchcock.

Alfred Hitchcock films *Torn Curtain*

Overleaf: Paul Newman, Julie Andrews and Lila Kedrova in *Torn Curtain*

Above: John Hodiak,
Walter Slezak, Tallulah
Bankhead, Hume Cronyn,
Henry Hull, Heather Angel
and Mary Anderson in
Lifeboat

Right: realistic ocean
waves in the studio tank
pounded the cast of
Lifeboat

Left: Paul Newman and
Ludwig Donath in *Torn
Curtain*

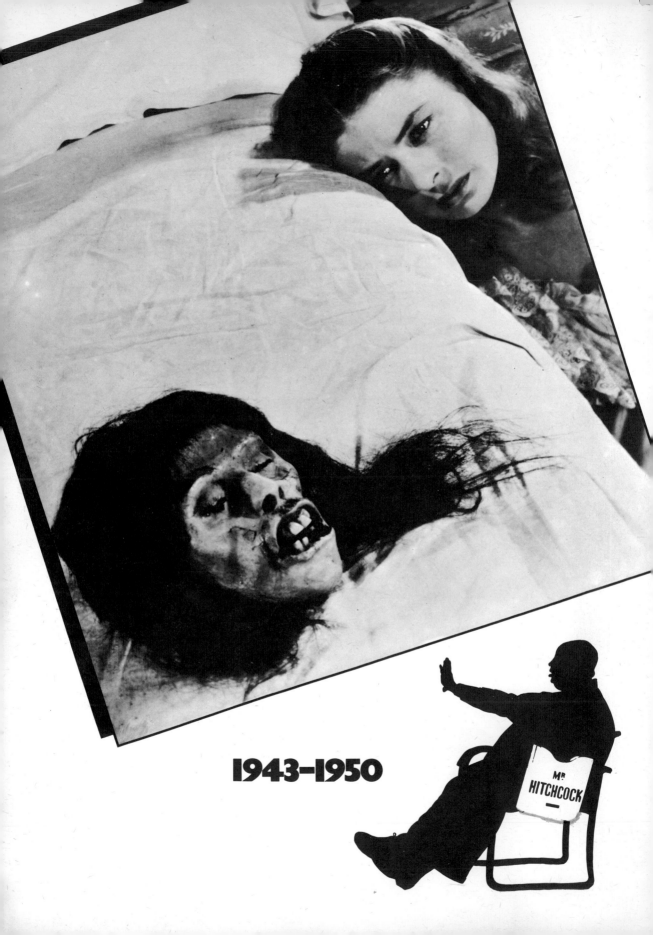

1943-1950

Although well over the age for military service Hitchcock was disappointed at not being able to make a direct contribution to the British war effort. At the end of 1943 he received his chance: an offer from Sidney Bernstein (now Lord Bernstein), who was at the wartime Ministry of Information, to make two films for showing in France on liberation with the intention of boosting morale should any mopping up of resisters be necessary. A group of French actors in London was brought together as the Molière Players, and both films were made in French, with no copies for the English-speaking world. The first one, *Bon Voyage*, concerned the escape across France of an R.A.F. officer in the company of a Pole working for the Resistance. But on reaching London he realizes he had really been a Gestapo agent.

The second film, like the first, was a four-reeler and was called *Aventure Malgache*. It was set in Madagascar after Pétain had ordered its capitulation to the Axis powers. For the two films Hitchcock was paid a nominal £10 a week. There was a possibility of his staying in Europe to make a film set in a prison camp, but it did not materialize and after ten months in wartime England he returned to Hollywood to fulfil his contract for David O. Selznick. He had agreed to make a film of Francis Beeding's novel, *The House of Dr Edwardes*.

The film was called *Spellbound* and starred Ingrid Bergman and Gregory Peck. It was produced at a time when the psychological drama was very much in vogue, and there were strong hints of satire at the expense of psychiatrists in Ben Hecht's screenplay. Peck played the new head of a mental home in a remote setting who turns out to be an impostor – an amnesiac to boot, guilt-ridden for having caused the death of an infant brother in childhood, who has somehow assumed the identity of the real doctor. He suspects that he has in fact killed him, but with the aid of a brilliant and glamorous female member of the institution's staff, Ingrid Bergman, he is able to unravel the mystery and unmask the real murderer. An injected highlight was a dream sequence devised by Salvador Dali, although the images that he produced were surprisingly unoriginal for the man who inspired *Un Chien Andalou*. Another device that was a gimmick and made no direct contribution to the story, was a suicide shown by a giant hand turning a revolver in close-up to confront the audience. The screen then erupted into a brilliant crimson flash (the film was in black and white). A glossy Miklos Rozsa score, with a surging, romantic theme tune, inevitably sentimentalized the love scenes, although the first kiss was shot in considerable style, with a series of doors opening in soft focus. Hitchcock felt that *Spellbound* was really a whodunit dressed up as a piece of psychiatric insight, and for all its complicated explanations – it is one of the wordiest of his films – it fails to convince.

Ben Hecht also scripted the next of his films, *Notorious*,

Ingrid Bergman suffers the torments inflicted by a jealous housekeeper in *Under Capricorn*

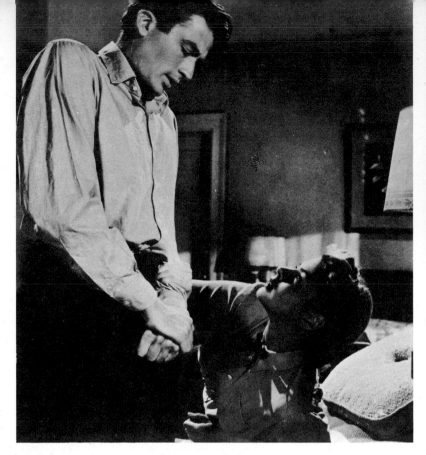

made at RKO. Ingrid Bergman was once again the heroine, and Cary Grant played opposite her with Claude Rains completing the triangle. Cary Grant was a much more relaxed and acceptable Hitchcock hero than the young Gregory Peck, whose acting had not lost its early stiffness at the time of the preceding picture.

The setting of *Notorious* was Rio de Janeiro, with Grant as Devlin, a U.S. secret service man tracking down a group of Nazis. He enlists the assistance of Alicia, played by Ingrid Bergman, the daughter of a convicted traitor who has killed himself in prison, and although she had no part in his activities she feels compelled to expiate his crimes. Devlin is wary at first but later falls in love with her. In order to get to their goal she marries Sebastian (Claude Rains), the leader of the Nazis and an old admirer. At a party after the wedding Devlin and Alicia find evidence in the wine cellar proving Sebastian's espionage activities, but with his suspicions aroused he begins a slow process of poisoning his bride. Finally Devlin carries her away from the house, carrying her prostrate form past her husband who is unable to stop him, but must later face the wrath and punishment of his fellow Nazis.

Particularly successful in the film was the interplay of the various characters. On the one hand the Grant hero was cool, cynical, carrying a chip on his shoulder, while Bergman was sensual, fond of fast cars, hard liquor and sex. In a sense she is

Left: Ingrid Bergman and Gregory Peck relive Peck's childhood trauma in the psychological thriller, *Spellbound*

Above: Hitchcock with his two leading players, Cary Grant and Ingrid Bergman, during an interlude in the filming of *Notorious*

expected to prostitute herself for the sake of the war effort, but her sacrifice earns from Grant a certain contempt as though she is confirming to him that she is just a whore. The Claude Rains character, like so many Hitchcock villains, is smooth, cultured, charming, sensitive and sympathetic: his slight build and gentle manner a distinct contrast to the boorish Grant. He is even under the thumb of a domineering mother, a most unusual situation in which to find a dangerous spy. It is the mother who is the impetus behind the poisoning of Alicia. At the film's conclusion the audience is made to feel a genuine concern for Sebastian's plight.

Notorious was photographed by Ted Tetzlaff in a stylish manner, with several superb sequences – a long, travelling embrace from the high terrace of a luxury apartment overlooking the Copacabana, the two players locked together as they go inside and Cary Grant takes a phone call. An almost vertical crane shot at the party takes in the general scene and then moves in on Ingrid Bergman from a great height; the camera seeking and finding the key to the wine cellar concealed tightly in her hand. This astonishing shot was of a similar technical virtuosity to the ballroom shot in *Young and Innocent* a decade earlier.

Later in the same sequence there was much suspenseful cross-cutting between the couple rooting about in their search for evidence in the cellar and diminishing stocks of champagne at the bar which will inevitably cause Sebastian to discover them as he goes down to replenish the bottle supply. During the poisoning sequence Ingrid Bergman, bed-ridden, was confronted with giant coffee cups filling the screen, an attention-winning trick that recalled the allegedly fatal glass of milk carried by Cary Grant to Joan Fontaine in *Suspicion* which was lit from within to give it an unnatural and emphatic glow.

An instance of unusual prescience occurred when Hitchcock selected his MacGuffin for *Notorious*. He felt that the commodity the spies should be interested in ought to be uranium, since it was the material from which an atomic bomb could be made. Since it was well before Hiroshima, and the Manhattan Project was the most closely guarded secret in the western hemisphere, Hitchcock's suggestion was regarded so seriously that he was actually put under surveillance by the F.B.I., although at the time he did not know it.

The contract with Selznick was concluded with *The Paradine Case*, from a novel by Robert Hichens, and with a script by Selznick himself. The result was a flaccid, ponderous, unsuccessful picture, an old-fashioned courtroom drama flawed by the miscasting of Gregory Peck as a barrister infatuated with a beautiful woman (Alida Valli) on trial for murdering her husband, and Louis Jourdan as a groom who was her lover. This latter part should have been filled by an actor who could suggest the dust and dirt of a stable clinging to him, but as Selznick had the actor under contract he insisted that he be used, even though he was something of a matinee idol. Charles Laughton was a happier choice as a sadistic judge whose cold indifference he acted with relish.

Hitchcock pursued his fascination for the trappings of law and order with lingering shots of Valli undergoing arrest and the formalities of being received into custody. That the impact of prison on someone of a higher social background is likely to be far more traumatic is another of his favourite preoccupations. Strangely, at the end of the film she is revealed as being guilty of her crime and the barrister is professionally disillusioned as the case blows up in his face, but at least his rocky marriage (to Ann Todd) is saved.

The film was made immediately after *Notorious*, but its showing in England was delayed until 1949 on account of the imposition of a 75 per cent *ad valorem* tax imposed by the British government in 1947 on all American films. This led in turn to a complete freeze on Hollywood products, only removed when the tax was rescinded in the following year, with a consequent logjam of new films awaiting screening.

Two technical innovations were made with Hitchcock's next film. *Rope* was his first to be made in colour. The second departure from his usual practice was far more drastic. He used the so-called 'ten-minute take' which allowed the action to continue for as long as there was enough film in the camera to record it. Reel changes were disguised by big close-ups of people's backs or other neutral surfaces, and the whole film flowed without the customary cuts and other instances of editing. The play by Patrick Hamilton on which the film was based preserved the unity of time by having all the action take place within the exact time span in which it took the story to be enacted. Hitchcock felt that the best way to convey this unity on the screen would be by shooting the whole film straight, without fades, dissolves or other opticals – and without cuts. No film had been made this way before, and none since, with the possible exceptions of Andy Warhol's *Sleep* and *Empire State*, which, however, make no attempt to tell a story.

The actors were rehearsed for weeks as though preparing a stage play, and gained sufficient proficiency to perform before the camera without interruption. The action was followed around by the camera which was like an extra spectator. There was only one setting, a luxurious penthouse apartment, high above New York, the Manhattan skyline boldly visible through the high windows at the back of the set, a skyscraper city seen in sunlight, dusk and finally night with every building twinkling with hundreds of lights. Somewhere in the night Hitchcock's silhouette appeared etched in neon to advertise his favourite mythical product, Reduco.

The plot concerned the murder by two young homosexuals

Above: Hitchcock makes his appearance in *The Paradine Case* behind his star, Gregory Peck

of one of their class members to demonstrate their Nietzschean superiority over their fellow men. They hide the body in a large chest in the apartment, in the very room in which a short time later they are entertaining their victim's parents, fiancée and tutor to cocktails. The college professor becomes suspicious and returns to confront them. He discovers the body and learns that his own carelessly spoken words have been used as a justification for the murder. After savagely denouncing the pair for distorting his vocal wisdom he throws open the window and whistles for the police.

John Dall and Farley Granger were convincing as the two murderers, recalling the infamous Leopold-Loeb case of the twenties, but James Stewart, furnished with greying temples, did not at the time quite have the presence to carry off a somewhat improbable and difficult part. The concept of the piece is essentially theatrical, and dramatic trickery that works well enough in the theatre sometimes falls flat in the more realistic medium of the cinema.

The technique of the film was fascinating, and the shooting of each reel must have been a terrifying experience, for walls, furniture, lights and ornaments were constantly being moved outside camera range to enable it to move around freely; every manoeuvre being accomplished by necessity in complete silence. The film took eighteen days to shoot, which meant that with ten reels six days' shooting was absolutely useless. The last reels were reshot because the sunset had been handled too brightly and was unconvincing. The skyline was an extremely elaborate work, complete with individually moving clouds, and lighting it was immensely difficult. Hitchcock made a number of discoveries about colour movies when he made *Rope*, the most significant being that Hollywood technicians lit for colour in exactly the same way as for black and white but with greater intensity. Thus they produced unconvincing effects, harsh shadows and strong hues where in reality they would be muted. It was, however, to take several more films in Technicolor before he was able to put his new-found knowledge to use.

The ten-minute take was, however, in spite of its technical ingenuity, an embarrassment; however logical it may have sounded in theory, in practice it just did not work. The action was slowed to the point of tedium and the effort required to avoid cuts seemed totally unjustified. It also ran counter to Hitchcock's professed beliefs in the power and necessity for cross-cutting in telling a story and creating suspense. Not surprisingly, he abandoned it for his next film, although there were still some vestiges remaining in *Under Capricorn*, but only in isolated scenes.

Like *Rope* this film was made in partnership with Sidney Bernstein, for a company they had formed, Transatlantic Pictures. The first film had been shot at the Warner Studios at

Below: Ann Todd and Charles Laughton in *The Paradine Case*

Above: Margaret Leighton, Michael Wilding, Joseph Cotten and Jack Watling in *Under Capricorn*, a costume melodrama set in New South Wales

Above left: *Rope* was filmed entirely on this set of a Manhattan apartment

Below left: The denouement in *Rope* as James Stewart fires into the night to bring the police

Overleaf: Marlene Dietrich as a musical star in *Stage Fright*

Inset: Michael Wilding, Jane Wyman, Alastair Sim and Sybil Thorndike in the same film

Burbank, but for *Under Capricorn* Hitchcock returned to England to make it at the MGM Studios at Borehamwood. It was his third costume picture, and like the lamentable *Waltzes from Vienna* and the implausible *Jamaica Inn* it offered confirmation that this was not Hitchcock's métier.

The action was set in Australia in the 1830s. Joseph Cotten played a former convict who had become wealthy, and was married to an alcoholic Irish aristocrat, Lady Henrietta, played by Ingrid Bergman. A cousin of the governor's nephew (Michael Wilding) is newly arrived from England. A jealous housekeeper (Margaret Leighton) has terrorized her mistress and provokes a confrontation between the two men which results in the cousin being wounded. Only a last minute confession by Lady Henrietta that she was responsible for the crime for which her husband was transported saves him from the gallows.

The melodramatic, yet slow-moving story, written by the Scottish playwright James Bridie from a novel by Helen Simpson, was a brave disappointment and perhaps an unfortunate choice of subject for Hitchcock's first film for ten years in the land of his birth. The careful colour photography by Jack Cardiff and the score by Richard Addinsell helped to give the film a slight veneer of worth, but the work as a whole is a baffling departure from the accepted idea of a Hitchcock picture. It was a box-office failure, and the production costs had been considerably increased by the high salary paid to Ingrid Bergman.

Under Capricorn is not entirely without admirers, however. The burden of guilt carried by several of the characters; the recurrence of the poisoning and alcohol theme from *Notorious*; the wicked housekeeper from *Rebecca* and the attraction of a high-born woman for a stableman as in *The Paradine Case* have provided convenient points of reference and comparison, especially in France. The leisurely tempo of the film has been regarded by Claude Chabrol and Erich Rohmer, with others of the *Cahiers du Cinema* group of critics, as masterly style rather than an ill-considered assemblage of Hitchcockian clichés in an inappropriate context.

Hitchcock made another film in England – a thriller that was in some ways reminiscent of his British films in the thirties, but whose attack failed to stand comparison. *Stage Fright* was hardly a simple whodunit, for the basic reason that the audience was given inaccurate information on which to base their deductions. A young man played by Richard Todd seeks out a girl friend who is training at the Royal Academy of Dramatic Art (Jane Wyman) and tells her that he is suspected of murdering the husband of a musical star (Marlene Dietrich) who was actually responsible. The girl agrees to put her acting skills to the test by impersonating a cockney maid in the star's house. An amorous Scotland Yard inspector (Michael Wilding) becomes involved in the case and the girl wards off his advances. An attempt to unmask the lady at a theatrical garden party ends in failure, and the final twist of the film reveals that the young man was the murderer all the time.

The reason that the audience could hardly be expected to reach this conclusion was because in a flashback Marlene Dietrich had been revealed as guilty, although the scene was intended to be shown as told by Richard Todd. It is a convention of films that flashbacks never lie – what is seen as action on the screen must have happened. The breaking of this rule marred the picture and was an uncharacteristic error of judgement on the part of the director. The presence of a number of box-office stars – Dietrich, Wyman (who had won an Oscar in the previous year), Wilding, Todd and Alastair Sim as the colourful and improbable father of Jane Wyman, did not lift the film out of a rut of mediocrity and it seemed that Hitchcock, now fifty-one, had lost his touch.

It was the end of the first decade in Hollywood, and during that period it appeared that the lightness, humour and pace of his thirties British films had become totally submerged and forgotten as bigger budgets and stars, and more pretentious stories, had lessened his invention. Already in that year of 1950 the epitaphs on his career were being written. But like so many things in the unpredictable business of film-making the valedictory noises were amazingly premature.

loss of praise

1951-1956

Just as in 1933 the dreadful *Waltzes from Vienna* was followed by the superb *The Man Who Knew Too Much*, Hitchcock, back at the Burbank studios, performed one of his most brilliant coups by making a film that was undoubtedly one of the three best in his long career. *Strangers on a Train* was from a novel by Patricia Highsmith, which had been adapted for the screen by Raymond Chandler, Czenzi Ormonde and Whitfield Cook.

It was a murder story of a chilling and ingenious kind. On a train a famous tennis player, Guy (Farley Granger), meets an affluent, loquacious fellow passenger, Bruno (Robert Walker), who in the course of the journey outlines a preposterous scheme whereby he will murder Guy's unpleasant wife, freeing him to marry a Senator's daughter, if Guy in turn will kill Bruno's autocratic father. Guy shrugs off the proposal, believing Bruno to be an eccentric, but learns with horror a few days later that his wife has been savagely murdered at a fairground, and owing to his own poor alibi the finger of suspicion is inevitably pointing in his direction. Bruno now approaches Guy, telling him that he has fulfilled his half of the bargain, and now it is for him to reciprocate, but Guy demurs. Bruno then threatens to plant Guy's lighter at the scene of the crime where the police will undoubtedly find it. Guy has to win an important tennis match, then race to the little town to stop Bruno from carrying out his threat. There is a spectacular struggle on an out-of-control merry-go-round between Guy and Bruno, ended when the whole structure crashes in a collapsed heap of twisted metal. Bruno dies, but not before making it clear to the onlookers that Guy is innocent.

With his return to America Hitchcock had got out into real locations, and *Strangers on a Train* had the convincing look of a film such as *Shadow of a Doubt*. The authentic backgrounds were used: Washington, the tennis courts, the record shop in which Guy's wife worked, the travelling fair – and not least the big trains, always regarded by Hitchcock with an almost schoolboy-like passion, and on which so much of the key action takes place.

There are riches for the Hitchcock enthusiast: the best example of the transference of guilt in all his pictures, with Guy rid of a wife he wanted dead and free to marry the woman of his choice, but feeling an intense sense of guilt for wanting such a situation, and for being unable to fulfil the reciprocal service for Bruno, who has absurdly become his benefactor. The murder is reflected in the victim's glasses – a slow strangulation on a deserted island at night, while across the lake the noises of the amusement park can be heard on the wind. Bruno's singularity is expressed in a magnificent shot of a tennis crowd, their heads swivelling to follow the ball, but with one head – Bruno's – stationary, intently smiling at Guy at his end of the court. Later there is an intensive cross-cutting

In a flashback in I Confess *Montgomery Clift has a brief love affair with Anne Baxter: here they are caught in a torrential summer rainstorm*

Right: Robert Walker and
Farley Granger fight to the
death in *Strangers on a
Train*, one of Hitchcock's
three best films

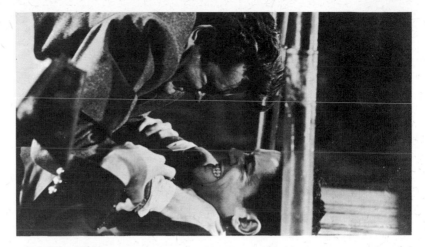

between Guy struggling to win his match and Bruno trying to
recover Guy's lighter from a grille he has accidentally dropped
it into, in the small town where he intends to plant it.

It was the first Hitchcock film of many to be photographed
by Robert Burks – a partnership that was to remain satisfactory
and fruitful. The next film was set in French Canada and
filmed mainly on location in the city and province of Quebec.
It was called *I Confess*, and in it, Montgomery Clift, not the
most likely Hitchcockian actor, played a priest who had heard
a confession to a murder, but was bound by his vows not
to reveal it to the authorities. He then found himself suspected of the crime and brought to trial, where he was acquit-
ted on the grounds of reasonable doubt, but hostile crowds
around the courthouse remained unconvinced. Finally the
murderer's wife broke the silence and was shot, the man
retreating to the vast Château Frontenac, where he was eventually cornered and shot down by the police, making his last
confession to the same priest.

I Confess is the closest that Hitchcock has got to a religious
subject, although it is a fairly straightforward thriller, the only
distinction being that the identity of the murderer is known
from the beginning and the suspense stems from the priest's
dilemma. It is harder for non-Catholics to accept the power of
the confessional and to some critics the situation appeared to
be far too contrived: it was unlikely that a priest would jeopar-
dize his own life to preserve the secrets told him. Catholics on
the other hand would not find the situation unacceptable.

For the searcher after Hitchcockian symbolism the film is a
happy hunting-ground, and the unusual setting of Quebec,
with its narrow, unfamiliar streets, religious statuary, scurry-
ing cassocked priests and ecclesiastical architecture offered
rich images. Hitchcock was not too happy about the casting of
Clift, who was a Method actor and therefore less able to take
his style of direction, but his performance was nonetheless
effective – dignified, tormented, yet contained. Hitchcock also

Left: Robert Walker closes
on his unsuspecting victim
(Laura Elliott) in *Strangers
on a Train*

wanted the Swedish actress Anita Bjork in the part taken by Anne Baxter; she was slightly at sea as the wife of a Member of Parliament who had been Clift's girlfriend before he was ordained. A beautifully composed flashback encapsulated their love affair. The chase through the Château Frontenac, while being a recognizable element in a Hitchcock film, seemed here out of character, as though he was unable to resist the temptation of providing a melodramatic climax.

After *I Confess* Hitchcock briefly flirted with a new technique of presentation – 3D. In 1953 the 3D craze had erupted as suddenly as the advent of sound a quarter of a century earlier, and many thought that the flat film was doomed. But the method of projection was extremely cumbersome, requiring separate prints on linked projectors and special Polaroid viewing glasses. Hence after a few months the bubble burst, and the unreleased 3D films went out in normal flat versions, Hitchcock's *Dial M for Murder* among them.

This was a straightforward adaptation by Frederick Knott of his successful stage play, and it was shot in colour. Hitchcock took the project on because at the time he was lacking a more ambitious subject, and he needed to keep his creative muscles flexed. He resisted the temptation to open up the film, and confined the action, for all but a couple of scenes, to a London flat. In it lives a retired tennis champion (Ray Milland) who is sponging off his rich wife (Grace Kelly). Knowing that

Above: On trial in *I Confess*, Montgomery Clift faces Brian Aherne, the prosecutor. The hero's dilemma was posed by the binding power of the confessional

Above right: Alfred Hitchcock

Right: Dany Robin, Frederick Stafford, Hitchcock, John Forsythe and Claude Jade– the cast of *Topaz* with their director

Overleaf: Alfred Hitchcock with Claude Jade and Dany Robin during the filming of *Topaz*

Left: Alfred Hitchcock

she is having an affair with an American writer (Robert Cummings) he decides to kill her to gain her fortune. The accomplice he hires is accidentally killed instead, and he resourcefully adapts his plan to make it seem that his wife is guilty. She is arrested, charged, tried, sentenced and all but executed before a wily inspector and her lover prove her innocence.

Dial M for Murder was very much a dialogue film, the camera holding heads in close-up and faithfully recording the cat-and-mouse exchanges. During the exposition of the murder plan the action is observed from overhead, producing an unusual angle and emphasizing the boxlike confinement of the set, representing a two-roomed flat, surprisingly small for a wealthy woman. Hitchcock exercised ingenuity in making his customary appearance, in this case as a diner at a formal banquet pictured in a photograph on the wall of the apartment.

Batteries recharged, his next film was a tour-de-force, an interesting study in latent voyeurism. *Rear Window* was another film in which the action was confined to a single apartment, but in this case it was in New York, overlooking a courtyard and a number of similar apartments in the building opposite. James Stewart played a photo-journalist resting after an accident getting a story. With his leg in a cast he is left moodily alone in his room by day, and spends his evenings grumbling to his attractive girlfriend (Grace Kelly). He begins to fantasize about his neighbours, watching them through a long lens as they go about their daily business. They fall into stereotypes – a Miss Lonelyhearts preparing to entertain admirers who never come, a trendy composer, a nymphomaniac chorus girl, newlyweds and so on. It occurs to him as he watches that one man could quite easily be a wife murderer and he begins to make aspects of his behaviour consistent with that theory. Eventually he realizes that the man has indeed murdered his wife, and moreover that he is aware that he has been discovered. Having convinced his girlfriend of the truth and exposed her to considerable danger he now finds that

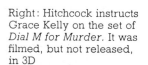

Right: Hitchcock instructs Grace Kelly on the set of *Dial M for Murder*. It was filmed, but not released, in 3D

Overleaf: Raymond Burr wraps the instruments with which he has dismembered his wife's corpse in *Rear Window*. He should have lowered the venetian blind

he himself is vulnerable to the man's attack. In the climax he is nearly murdered, and gets his other leg broken.

Although the setting is restricted it is a very cinematic work, and as Hitchcock pointed out to François Truffaut, one part of the film is the view of an immobilized man looking out, the other part is how he reacts; this being the purest expression of a cinematic idea. We are all voyeurs, we like to watch without being seen – but emerging from this idea is an even more Olympian one; we want to manipulate events, leave our mark in some way. James Stewart actually wants the man to be a wife murderer because it will fit in with the premise he has created, and consequently he is willing the death of an innocent woman. He is, therefore, to some extent guilty.

As so often in Hitchcock's films the hero is not particularly likeable – there is an arrogant, deprecating scorn in his view of the lives of those around him, and his fiancée is brittle, impatient and anxious to ensnare him. He in turn nearly gets her killed in order to prove the validity of his obsessive belief. Hitchcock has often stated that there is no murder like an English murder, and his encyclopaedic knowledge of criminology was put to good use. The crime in this film, although transferred from Holloway to Greenwich Village, is clearly based on that of Dr Crippen, who was also caught after the neighbours had become suspicious.

Rear Window is a stunning technical achievement, a black comedy glimpse of life and a revelation of Hitchcockian misanthropy, revealing how basically sordid many human instincts can be. Like most of his films from now on it was shot in colour; in fact, he was to use black and white only twice more, for *The Wrong Man* and *Psycho*.

To Catch a Thief was a lighter effort, written by the screenwriter of *Rear Window*, John Michael Hayes, and set on the French Riviera. Cary Grant improbably played an expert jewel thief, enjoying a well-earned retirement in the sun, who is suspected when a series of robberies performed in his style takes place along the coast. Grace Kelly played a wealthy American girl, with an ice-cool exterior waiting to be melted. There is for her vicarious pleasure in the possibility that the man she fancies is really the thief, but the denouement, which takes place at a costume ball held in lavish style, discloses that the robber is in fact another girl. The photography was lush, romantic and as colourful as a travel poster. In one sequence a chase takes place in a flower market; in another two cars race in pursuit along the Corniche, filmed from high above by helicopter.

Hitchcockian jokes abound – one particularly revolting shock comes when the vulgar mother of Grace Kelly, played extravagantly by Jessie Royce Landis, stubs out her cigarette in a fried egg. Hitchcock's dislike of eggs is well known. Red herrings, false trails, non sequiturs are in profusion, but when

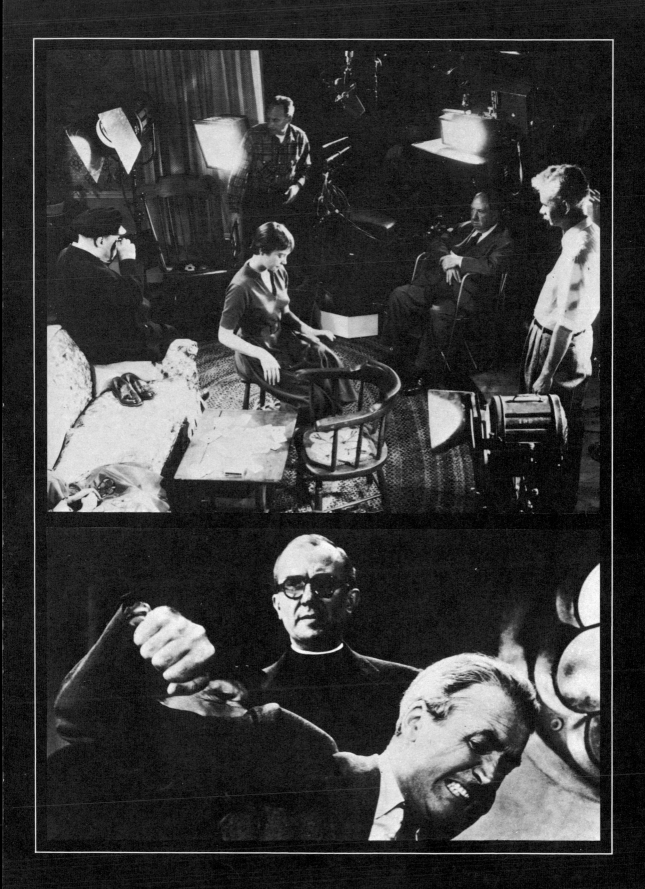

they are eliminated it is a simple chase story. Grace Kelly admirably portrayed Hitchcock's favourite kind of sexuality, where a cool, bland, poised outward appearance conceals an almost unbridled passionate drive within. At the end of the film she gets her man, then delivers the body blow by telling him that mother will be living with them too.

By the time that he began filming *The Trouble With Harry*, Hitchcock had become involved with television. From 1955 to 1965 he produced more than 350 half-hour and, later, one-hour films in the series *Alfred Hitchcock Presents*, and of these he directed a score himself. All were preceded by a humorous introduction, delivered as a monologue to the camera, after his corpulent figure had filled an outline profile in time with a whimsical signature tune. These prologues, uttered by Hitchcock in his unique rasping stage cockney, quickly established him as one of the most readily identifiable television personalities and a gift for impressionists. Although shot over a period rarely exceeding three days, some of the television films were minor classics of their kind, encapsulating Hitchcockian themes successfully within a constricted framework.

The Trouble With Harry, although not successful with the public, was one of Hitchcock's best forays into black comedy, a film about a troublesome corpse. It teetered precariously on the edge of bad taste in the best tradition of the genre. Set in the woods of Vermont during the richly-hued beauty of the New England autumn, Harry's body is discovered one morning by a small boy. During the course of the day numerous people have reason to believe that they are the cause of Harry's demise, either by accident or design, and his body becomes a macabre prop to be buried, dug up, reinterred, hidden and discovered at frequent intervals. His face is never seen, but his shoeless feet, either bare or garbed in vivid socks, dominate the action.

Shirley MacLaine in an early screen role plays Harry's young, estranged wife, Mildred Natwick an ageing spinster, Edmund Gwenn, making a Hitchcockian reappearance after many years, a retired sea captain (who to his shame has done nothing more exciting than skippering a tug on the East River) and John Forsythe, the romantic interest for Shirley MacLaine, a young abstract artist. The screenplay was again by John Michael Hayes, from a novel by Jack Trevor Story. Hitchcock had overturned the cliché, dragging his black melodrama out of the shadows into the golden sunlight of a Vermont autumn, thus sanitizing the distasteful element of the plot, namely that its central character is a cadaver in the grip of *rigor mortis*. The audience is brought into the joke with a nudging, winking complicity. The understated attitude towards the corpse was well illustrated with the memorable line Mildred Natwick delivered to a perspiring Edmund Gwenn as he very obviously struggled to pull Harry by the legs across rough ground: 'What seems to be the trouble, Captain?'

Above: Hitchcock on set with Shirley Maclaine in *The Trouble with Harry*. It was her first film

Below: James Stewart is seized in *The Man Who Knew Too Much*, as Bernard Miles as a bogus preacher looks on

1956–1960

itchcock then turned to one of his classic films of the thirties and made a new version of it, using colour and VistaVision, forty-five minutes extra playing time, and two eminent box-office stars in the parts originally taken by Edna Best and Leslie Banks – Doris Day and James Stewart. Curiously, in spite of the extra length two major scenes were missing in the remake: that at the dentist's surgery where the hero turns the tables on the villain by dosing him with his own gas, and the street siege sequence. The 1934 version of *The Man Who Knew Too Much* was set in St Moritz, but now the scene was shifted to Marrakesh, a geographical displacement that appeared to be serving the needs of Technicolor rather than plot. The famous Royal Albert Hall sequence was shot much more ambitiously, with even the original cantata reorchestrated and furnished with superior musicianship. Said Hitchcock himself in *The Times* eight years after the film was released: 'When I made the second version (which was perhaps not a good idea anyway, but I wanted a vehicle for James Stewart quickly, and it was just lying to hand) I found that most of the trouble was filling gaps in the story which no one in his right mind would want filled anyway, except that people would complain if all these inessentials were not spelled out.'

Other changes took note of the special talents of the new cast. Doris Day, the mother of a small boy this time, was a retired musical comedy actress, which gave her sufficient excuse to warble the anodyne lullaby 'Que Sera Sera (Whatever Will Be, Will Be)'. James Stewart was cast as a professional man, a doctor, giving his role slightly more colour than when Leslie Banks played it. The Albert Hall scenes were lengthier and greatly improved by better production values – it was as though Hitchcock having cherished the sequence for twenty-two years was able to leap at the opportunity of reworking it. Now he was able to do the things he was unable to do the first time – panning the camera along the actual score on the conductor's rostrum, for instance, towards the note indicating the fatal cymbal clash.

But gone was the spirit of freshness present in the original, for the scene had in itself become a cinematic cliché, and even Doris Day's histrionic agitation, and the frustrations of James Stewart in trying to convince the police of the imminent fulfilment of the assassination plot, lost the knife-edge suspense of the earlier film. Brenda de Banzie and Bernard Miles made an interesting pair of unlikely anarchists, while Daniel Gelin met his doom in the casbah, garbed as an Arab with brown boot polish on his face. Once again John Michael Hayes had worked on the screenplay, this time with Angus McPhail, who had worked on *Spellbound* and the two short wartime films for the Ministry of Information, but they were treading carefully in the steps of Charles Bennett and

James Stewart with Kim Novak in *Vertigo.* It was one of Novak's most effective performances, as a girl whose mysterious attributes seem to include a form of reincarnation

D. B. Wyndham-Lewis, the writers of the 1934 screenplay.

The Wrong Man represented a change of mood, to a real-life story shot on location in black and white. It was based on a genuine case of wrongful arrest, with Henry Fonda playing a night-club bass player picked up on suspicion of being a bank hold-up man. After being charged he was falsely identified and it was found that his handwriting showed similarities with the note used in the robbery. As the weight of circumstantial evidence piled up and he faced trial, his wife went mad and had to be placed in an institution. The only two witnesses who could have positively established his innocence died. Eventually the real robber committed another crime, was arrested and confessed. The wrong man was released, his life ruined, his wife probably permanently unbalanced. Hitchcock was tempted by this story he had read in a national magazine. It seemed to crystallize his fear of the machinery of the law and of the technical details of imprisonment; the horror multiplied if the victim of the law also happens to be innocent. So he took for him the unusual course of aiming at documentary realism. Following the original events closely, he was handicapped by the coincidences and dramatic loose ends that tend to make real life so untidy, and the film was further marred by the shift of emphasis from the musician, played by Henry Fonda, to his wife, Vera Miles, two-thirds of the way through the picture.

There is a considerable degree of Hitchcockery – the transfer of guilt as the wife begins to blame herself for what has happened, the meticulous observation of the processes of arrest and detention, the fingerprinting, handcuffing, locking-up. The policemen performing the arrest are not presented as malicious sadists, but as tired, overworked, underpaid men who have heard protestations of innocence from everybody they have arrested and are not prepared to make

The old dark house with dreadful secrets in *Psycho*. Tourists at Universal City can still visit this fine example of Californian gingerbread on the backlot

Cary Grant was a very acceptable hero, an adman who is mistaken in a New York hotel for an agent of the American government; Eva Marie Saint was a spies' moll who turns out to be on the side of the angels after all, and James Mason was at his oiliest as a suave foreign master spy. In one sequence there is an assassination at the United Nations Building in New York, and in another, probably one of the most famous scenes in any Hitchcock movie, Cary Grant is strafed by a low-flying crop-dusting plane in the middle of an open prairie. To create this astonishing piece of cinema Hitchcock deliberately stood the cliché on end by choosing the most open, exposed and unlikely setting for an ambush – a place far removed from the traditional dark alleyways, gleaming cobblestones and hidden doorways of orthodox skulduggery.

The screenplay by Ernest Lehman was an original, not adapted from a novel or play, and is a model of suspense screenwriting, even if the plot becomes totally incomprehensible almost at once. The MacGuffins are shrugged off in the best Hitchcockian manner – Leo G. Carroll as a blasé intelligence chief refuses to specify his exact agency, by saying: 'F.B.I. . . . C.I.A. . . . O.N.I. . . . we're all in the same alphabet soup,' while James Mason's villainy is explained in the simple statement that his men are after government secrets. None of it matters for the film is superb, fast-moving entertainment from start to finish, shot with a polished assurance, rich in humour and irony as well as menace and excitement. It is a fitting final word on the chase theme, and a perfect summation of Hitchcock's experience in making this kind of picture.

Having disposed of the chase he now turned to the Old Dark House and set to the task of making the definitive film within this genre. The resulting work was one of his undoubted masterpieces. *Psycho* was in some respects a horror comic, an E. C. Gaines macabre adventure, and it was never meant to be taken as seriously as the contemporary British film critics insisted on regarding it. They were affronted, believing that Hitchcock had been subverted by his weekly television show into an exhibition of bad taste. Audiences were far more perceptive, and the film was an outstanding commercial success.

The opening was precise, a title establishing date, time and place. A secretary absconds with a bankroll, stolen from the office in which she works as a trusted employee, and sets out on a long car journey to join her lover in another city. After an exhausting drive through heavy rain, and a mysterious encounter with a policeman who may or may not have been suspicious, she decides to check in for the night at a lonely wayside motel, where the young proprietor, a gentle, shy man, reveals his interest in taxidermized birds and the presence of an aged, possessive, invalid mother who lives in the ginger-bread gothic house overlooking the site. During the night, while the girl is taking a shower, someone enters the cabin and stabs her to death. It is, it would seem, the old woman. The son then appears to mop up the blood and carry the body to the boot of the car, driving it to a nearby swamp where it is submerged. The girl's sister and an insurance investigator get on the trail and arrive at the motel. While snooping around the house the man is savagely murdered. But eventually the mystery of the Bates Motel is solved – the old woman has been dead for years, but the psychopathic proprietor has partly assumed her personality and has been responsible for the murders. In the last scene a psychiatrist offers an explanation, while the murderer regresses into total lunacy.

Janet Leigh, the girl murdered in the shower, only appears in the first part of the film, an astonishingly rapid disposal of a major star. The shower sequence is horrifying on the screen, the victim repeatedly stabbed by a descending dagger, although no actual wounds are visible. The second murder, when the insurance investigator, played by Martin Balsam, is attacked as he ascends the staircase in the old house, is shot in such a way that audiences involuntarily gasp or shudder at its frightening suddenness. As he nears the top step an overhead shot shows a figure rushing from a door on the landing clutching the same weapon used in the shower. The unfortunate man is stabbed, and blood cascades down his temple as the camera follows him in close-up falling backwards down the stairs. At the bottom the assailant, who has followed, rains repeated wounds until he is dead. The sequence is accompanied by a terrifying musical chord, repeated over and over again like a demonic shriek.

Psycho was a relatively cheap film to make, and was shot in black and white, to a certain extent using techniques learned from the *Alfred Hitchcock Presents* television series, including the substitution of his chief television cameraman, John L. Russell, in place of Robert Burks. It was relatively the biggest-grossing of all Hitchcock's films.

Overleaf: The mouth of Janet Leigh in *Psycho,* as she is stabbed to death in the shower

Inset: Anthony Perkins, the owner of the motel and keen ornithologist

101

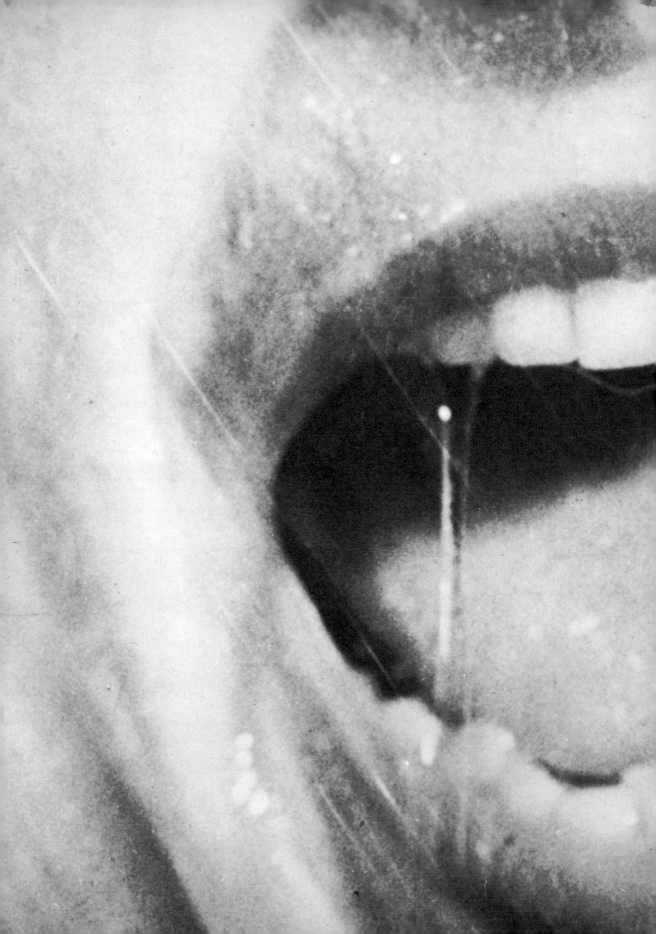

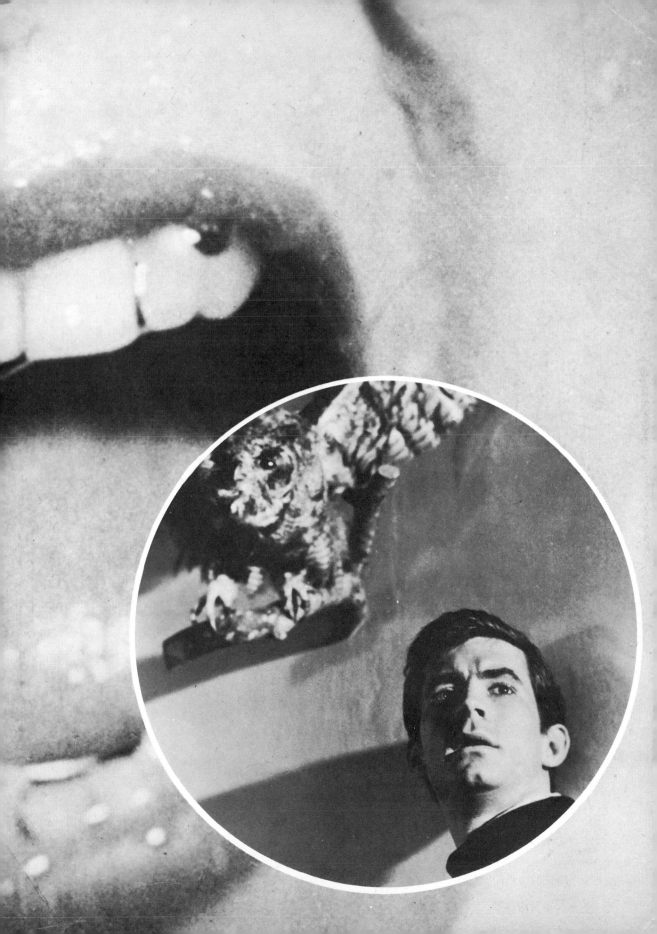

1961-

There was a break in his output following *Psycho*. Hitchcock was now well over sixty and heavily engaged in the television series which had viewers throughout the world. Finding a subject for a new film took time. Eventually, it turned out to be a work of Daphne du Maurier who had already furnished Hitchcock with two stories. *The Birds* was, however, a very different tale from either *Jamaica Inn* or *Rebecca*. Considerable technical problems had to be surmounted in order to transfer the novella from the printed page to the screen. *The Birds* described an ecological nightmare, a massive shift in the balance of nature which occurs when for some unspecified reason the bird population of the world turns against man. Hitchcock transferred the setting from England to northern California and compressed the action into a few days. *and this makes the movie intensed*

His main characters were an arrogant rich girl, accustomed through life to getting what she wants whenever she asks for it, and a sharp young lawyer who, in the opening sequence set in downtown San Francisco, pretends to be an assistant in a pet shop and scores several points off her. Flushed with the spirit of revenge and a certain interest in his confidence the girl tracks him down to his weekend lair, the home of his mother in a country fishing village, Bodega Bay, some miles north of the city. She drives up there, ready to develop the relationship, but on her way to the house she is attacked by a gull which cuts her head open. Shortly afterwards the inhabitants of Bodega Bay begin to experience disquieting unrest among the bird population. A children's party is brought to an abrupt end by a concerted bird strike and later they erupt in startling numbers through every window and opening in the house, even the chimney. It is not birds of prey, either, that are behaving in an aggressive manner, but the common species. In the morning it is discovered that an isolated farmhouse has been laid waste by the birds and the farmer killed. The children are chased from the village school, and shortly afterwards the whole community is under siege from a gull strike, during which a filling station blows up, reducing Bodega Bay to a shambles. The schoolmistress, who had been in love with the lawyer, is found dead. The sophisticated girl from San Francisco is savaged by an atticful of birds and unhinged by the experience is gently helped away from the house by the man and his mother. They drive off through a desolate landscape that has been taken over by the feathered species.

It is a parable, expressing Hitchcock's frequently voiced contention that it is in the ordinary things around us that menace and danger lurk, and perhaps our ultimate destruction. Never in his films has he come so close to portraying the ultimate cataclysm, the annihilation of the world by uncontrollable forces. It is one of his most stunning films, both in the development of the story, from a light-hearted mood of sophis-

Rod Taylor comforts a distressed Jessica Tandy in *The Birds* after her house has been laid waste by a feathered invasion

ticated comedy to the final horror, and in the technical ingenuity which went into the organization of the bird shots, with unusually complicated matte-work, much patient bird training and considerable fortitude on the part of the actors.

The principals were lesser-known performers – the man, Rod Taylor, an actor in the Cary Grant mould, but without the assurance, and Tippi Hedren, a tall and elegant blonde with a passive face, a former model with little acting experience. The blandness of the couple was to some extent mitigated by the casting of Jessica Tandy as the mother and Suzanne Pleshette as the schoolmistress, but it is evident that the director's main interest lies with the birds, and the humans are deliberately empty and superficial. There is a telling scene in the village restaurant when a middle-aged woman ornithologist, who just happens to be there after the schoolchildren have been attacked, pooh-poohs the whole notion of the bird world becoming aggressive because it goes against their nature, and later is forced to eat her words when the same building is besieged by gulls, with a grandstand view of the destruction outside. In the same scene a frightened mother rounds on the rich girl, accusing her of witchcraft and making all the terrible things happen by her presence in the village. It is certainly true that she is suffering guilt from her awakening: the vapid, useless and frivolous former existence as a socialite and playgirl behind her. There is no music in the film, only orchestrated bird effects by Bernard Herrman.

The supreme publicist, Hitchcock coined his own slogan to promote the film, and the curious syntax of the phrase 'The birds is coming!' helped to pull in his audiences.

The next was *Marnie*, a project he had attempted earlier when he had tried to lure the former Grace Kelly back to the screen. As Princess Grace of Monaco she found that the notion of a resumption of her screen career was not well-regarded by her husband's subjects, and discussions ceased. Tippi Hedren was now cast in the role of a girl who was a compulsive thief. The original novel was by Winston Graham, and it was adapted for the screen by J. Presson Allen. Cast in the role of a wealthy publisher who marries her was Sean Connery – on the face of it a strange choice, for he had already become slightly typecast by the James Bond image. *Marnie* ventured into *Spellbound* territory, the psychological thriller where a childhood trauma has affected the outlook of the adult. Marnie steals as a result of a psychotic disturbance, achieving with her efficient, respectable manner positions of trust, and then decamping with the contents of the office safe, to another city with a new name and a fresh shade of hair. Mark Rutland (Sean Connery) discovers that she has stolen the firm's money, confronts her and makes her agree to marry him or be handed over to the police. He is fascinated by the thought of being in love with a thief, and the strange power the situation gives him.

Above: Tippi Hedren and Rod Taylor pick their way through the carcass-littered town. This scene was cut from *The Birds*

Below: Chaos after a bird strike in the same film

Inevitably it is an unhappy marriage – the bride is frigid on her honeymoon and tries to kill herself. On the return to the ancestral acres she discovers that her sister-in-law spies on her and is intensely hostile. A disaster occurs when one of Marnie's former employers and victims visits the house and recognizes her. Her husband insists that with the money returned they can bluff their way through. The next day during a fashionable hunt there is an accident in which her favourite horse is killed and in a state of shock she drives into town to make another attempt on the Rutland safe. This time her husband catches up with her and drives her to Baltimore where in a dingy house near the waterfront his private detective has located her mother. The story of her childhood is pieced together – in wartime her mother, now obsessively strait-laced, had been a prostitute, and the five-year-old child had killed a sailor with a poker to stop her from being attacked; the incident had left no trace on Marnie's conscious memory.

The opening of *Marnie* was one of Hitchcock's best – a close-up of a big yellow bag, the camera pulling back to reveal it under a woman's arm; the background, a railroad station. Then cut to a close-up of an angry man in an office snarling: 'Robbed!' Then back to the girl, now in a hotel, transferring items from one case to another and the cash from the yellow bag. Then she rinses her hair, and only when she has finished do we see her face for the first time – the blonde Tippi Hedren. There are many extraordinary instances of visual power – Hitchcock's use of thunderstorms, heavy rain and the consequent rigours of driving through downpours; the camera distortion during the flashback recalling the childhood killing, where desaturated colour is combined with a rippling image; the colour effect on the screen when Marnie is confronted by red – with its disturbing effect on her subconscious.

The Baltimore street set was marred by a crudely-painted backdrop of a ship tied up at the end of the block, and much critical energy was spent in trying to fathom Hitchcock's intention. This was characteristically dispelled during a John Player Lecture at the National Film Theatre, London when in answer to a cineaste's long-winded question on this point he said that it had no significance: it was just a rotten piece of scene painting. Hitchcock has often been amused at the speculation by commentators on his motives, but his genius is often instinctive, things falling into place in his films because in his bones he has known that it would make good cinema in such a way. No film-maker can match him in the care of pre-production planning and it is one of the reasons why he is a master storyteller on film.

Marnie is an interesting work, with many echoes from earlier pictures – *Spellbound*, *Rebecca*, *Suspicion* and *Psycho*, where the theft, the rainstorm driving and the unsettling appearance of an unexplained man at a racetrack (as disquiet-

Hitchcock with Sean
Connery on the set of
Marnie

good point!

ing as the episode with the policeman in the earlier film) are all
paralleled. There was a deficiency of casting – the acting range
of Miss Hedren and the unbelievability of Sean Connery's
social position lessened credibility to some extent, although it
is arguable that neither were as they pretended to be – Connery
played a man who was in a sense as sick as Marnie, for he
wanted to be in love with a flawed person in order that he could
indulge in amateur psychiatry.

Unfortunate casting was a burden in the next film, released
in 1966. *Torn Curtain* was a return to the spy scene, but its
atmosphere was drab and jaded in comparison with its rum-
bustious predecessors. It was a pity that Hitchcock's hope to
make a return to Buchan with a film of *The Three Hostages*,
which would have brought the Richard Hannay character
back to the screen, came to nothing. *Torn Curtain* was written
by Brian Moore, and in it, Paul Newman, hardly a Hitchcockian actor (although he had played in an imitation, Mark
Robson's *The Prize*, which had purloined several Hitchcock
ideas), was now cast as an atomic physicist who has to pretend
to defect to East Germany in order to extract a secret scientific
formula. His fiancée, unaware of the deception, sets out to
find him and bring him back to the west. The couple are then
caught up in a series of adventures as they attempt to get out
from behind the Iron Curtain, some macabre, such as the
elimination of one of the Communist pursuers in a remote

Paul Newman finds killing a man not only distasteful but difficult in *Torn Curtain*, a thriller set partially in East Germany

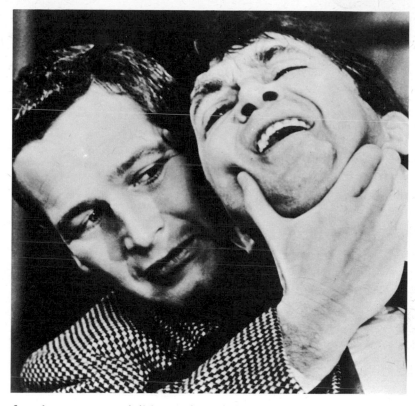

Overleaf
Above left: Hitchcock with Julie Andrews and Paul Newman on the set of *Torn Curtain*

Below left: A most effective sequence in *Topaz* was based on Fidel Castro's visit to New York when he stayed in unstatesmanlike Harlem

Right: Alfred Hitchcock

farmhouse, some risible, such as the sequence in a state theatre. Hitchcock seems to have been inspired by the Burgess and Maclean story and had offered his own spectacular embroidery on the theme. His heroine was improbably played by the rosy-cheeked Julie Andrews, fresh from triumphs in *Mary Poppins* and *The Sound of Music*, and although on her own terms she had been capable of reasonable performances, the juxtaposition of her and Paul Newman not only strained dramatic credibility but produced uneven, patchy acting.

In the farmhouse killing Hitchcock's intention was to show that the act of putting a man to death was in fact an exceedingly difficult task to accomplish, and by no means the quick, clean affair constantly portrayed on the screen. The hero, assisted by the farmer's wife, beat the man who was menacing them over the head with a shovel, poured hot soup straight from the stove over him, attacked him with a kitchen knife and finally pushed him into the gas oven. The sequence was extended and enacted without any music, heightening its horrific impact.

Torn Curtain was photographed by John F. Warren, using an interesting colour technique with minimal lighting. Consequently a deliberately severe effect was achieved, with restrained colour values and large, flat, monochromatic surfaces often visible. Although some of the background scenes had been shot in Germany there was, however, a strangely unconvincing atmosphere, too much of an off-target attempt to

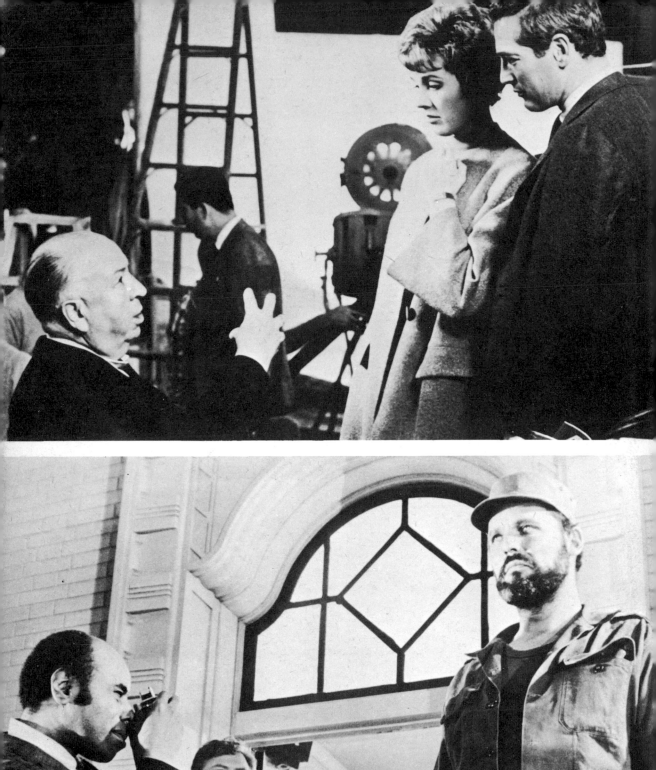

Above left: Michael Bates,
Alec McCowan and Vivien
Merchant in the same film

Below left: A nude body on
the highway in *Frenzy*

be put down as mere stylization, and *Torn Curtain* is not a particularly satisfying work.

The next Hitchcock film was *Topaz*, adapted from the best-selling novel by Leon Uris, about a French agent who helps the Americans in discovering the extent of the missile bases in Cuba. The film falls into two distinct parts. The first, set in Cuba, reaches its climax with the killing of the agent's girl friend (Karin Dor) in a beautifully-staged scene in the hallway of her house, her body gently tumbling to the floor from the fatal wound. The second is set in France, where Communist spies are uncovered in high places, and where the hero eventually unmasks Topaz. Frederick Stafford was a curiously unglamorous choice for a leading man, and stood barely a chance against the dashing performance of John Vernon as the Cuban leader. The best sequence in the film was based on Castro's famous visit to New York in which he and his entourage eschewed the bright lights of midtown Manhattan and deliberately stayed at a dingy hotel in Harlem.

Topaz is again not a wholly satisfactory work, and the fact that there was some confusion over the ending indicated a certain loss of confidence on Hitchcock's part, in that at this stage of his career he could still be victim to the whims of the front office. Two versions of the ending were actually seen in London. In one the unmasked agent returns to his Paris home, closes the front door behind him, the camera staying outside;

Right: Frederick Stafford
and Karin Dor in *Topaz*, a
spy thriller set in Cuba,
New York and France,
based on the book by Leon
Uris

113

shortly afterwards a shot is heard indicating that he has killed himself. In the alternative he is put on a plane for eastern Europe. Uncertainty of this kind carried beyond the first public showings of a film are rare and hard to excuse.

Now well past seventy, Hitchcock returned to England to make a murder film with all the trappings of his past career embedded in it. *Frenzy* in some respects harked back even beyond his Gaumont-British period, being in certain aspects reminiscent of *The Lodger* in its treatment. The shock opening, for instance, in which the disquiet felt by the female population of London at the presence of an unknown strangler of blondes at large is dramatized by the appearance of a floating nude body during a riverside ceremony in front of County Hall, is similar in effect to the opening of the 1926 film.

Hitchcock made a couple of errors in *Frenzy* of a kind that had got him into trouble in previous films. The first was to make his hero, played by Jon Finch, not only dislikeable but almost certainly spurious. He boasts, for instance, of a wartime R.A.F. record, although the film is clearly set in London in the seventies, which would have meant at the most optimistic that he had been a squadron leader at the age of 10. The second mistake was to reveal the identity of the killer too soon, thus removing much of the suspense of the story, and since Jon Finch plays an unsympathetic character with disturbing ambiguities, it might have been better to have taken the audience further down the garden path. The killer, played by Barry Foster, is for once a thoroughly unpleasant psychotic homosexual which to some extent forces sympathy against him, but the best performances are the supporting ones: Alec McCowan as a patient police detective saddled with a socially-conscious gourmet wife who is constantly serving him with unpalatable snob food, played by Vivien Merchant, and Anna Massey as the most appealing of the victims.

There is a certain amount of black comedy – the hiding, for instance, of a body in a sack of potatoes on the back of a loaded truck, with a bare foot constantly exposing itself. In spite of the nudity and frank dialogue *Frenzy* is a very old-fashioned film, and Anthony Shaffer's screenplay is over-literate and unconvincing. The use of London locations, particularly Covent Garden in its last days as a fruit market, was effective and there were many signs of the old Hitchcock, as imaginative and inventive as ever, even if the overall effort fell short of his best. It was his 52nd film in fifty years, a creditable score in a long life of film-making, and by no means an unworthy swansong. At the time of writing Ernest Lehman, who wrote the screenplay of *North by Northwest*, is adapting a thriller by Victor Canning for Hitchcock to start filming in late 1974 – encouraging news for his devotees.

Hitchcock has always considered himself primarily a storyteller with film: an entertainer, a showman. He has quite calculatedly restricted himself in his choice of subject matter,

Left: Hitchcock directs a scene from *Topaz*

avoiding epics, westerns, musicals and historical biographies, preferring to go for close-ups of the human predicament, which in his terms, comes down to menace from dark but hidden powers, be they the psychosis of the murderer or the paranoia lurking within apparently normal people. It is almost axiomatic that when he has strayed from his narrowly defined territory the result has been failure, whether it be the ponderous inappropriateness of *Waltzes from Vienna* or the dreary improbability of *Jamaica Inn*. There is in his approach to the craft a studied care and precision which have invariably given his films a distinctive polish. His pre-planning capacity is legendary. Before a single frame of film is exposed he will have gone over the script repeatedly, rejecting, rewriting, rejigging. He does not improvise on the floor. His actors will have rehearsed their roles to perfection, his cameraman will know exactly what is required. 'My films are made on paper,' is his significant remark when asked about his method. He has no need to look through the viewfinder.

It has been argued that with the modern style of film-making, which tends to be freer, more flexible, more improvisational, Hitchcock has been left stranded. It ignores the fact many of today's methods were tried by him many years ago, such as the improvised scenes in *Murder* and the overlapping sound in *Shadow of a Doubt*. Hitchcock has never been afraid to innovate, but has equally been ready to discard those ideas that do not work for him. The ten-minute take in *Rope*, while not being wholly successful, was technically an extraordinary achievement, and with superior equipment available today might have been a major breakthrough in assembling films. The principle is, after all, not that far different from the method used to videotape a television play.

But it is in the strength of narrative that Hitchcock is unexcelled. Because his films always tend to revolve around a basic confrontation of good and evil there are clear signposts for his audiences to follow, even if they are semi-literate. When the simplistic situation is obfuscated deliberately, either by making the villain more likeable than the hero as, for instance, in *The Secret Agent* or *Foreign Correspondent*, or by providing the hero with sufficient guilt to make him assume a burden of culpability as James Stewart in *Rear Window* and *Vertigo*, or Farley Granger in *Strangers on a Train*, this premise still holds – the drama is spiced as it were with the vicarious frisson of ambiguity which is almost a Hitchcockian stock in trade.

The French critics were the first to become acutely aware of the influences in his work directly derived from his Catholic faith – as would be expected. Apart from the most obvious examples, as when in such pictures as *I Confess, The Wrong Man* and *Vertigo* explicit reference is made to either churches or prayer, there are, particularly in the matter of assumed guilt, pronounced Catholic traits. The torment of the hero

Jon Finch and Barry Foster in *Frenzy*. In many ways it was reminiscent of *The Lodger*

frequently suggests a religious atonement, a redemption is sought that can only be worked out on his own, since the authorities are usually hostile or unable to help him. In many films the question occurs: 'Why doesn't he just tell the police?' But putting aside Hitchcock's celebrated distrust of blinkered authority, there is invariably good reason why the hero is not going to be believed – a predicament carried to its conclusion with Henry Fonda's treatment in *The Wrong Man*. Then there is the presence of disguised evil – the plausible villains, who by outward charm and respectability have achieved positions of high regard, as in *The Thirty Nine Steps* (Pauline Kael has noted how like Franklin D. Roosevelt is Godfrey Tearle as the master spy), *Jamaica Inn, Saboteur, Notorious, North by Northwest* and others. This is a demonstration of the deviousness of the Devil, the extent to which he can blind others to his presence and his outrageous resourcefulness.

Fear is a potent force in the Hitchcock armoury of effects, and the totally unexpected or unlikely eruption of danger and menace, another trademark. In a Hitchcock film the most ordinary setting must be treated with suspicion because there may well be something unpleasant lurking just out of sight. An innocent shopping bag can contain a loaded revolver, an open prairie could be the scene of a deadly attack, the haven of safety might turn out to be a viper's nest. Nothing can be taken for granted, nothing is what it seems. It is this unsettling

tension that has made him the master of suspense – the audience is constantly keyed, waiting for something to happen, but never really quite sure what. When Martin Balsam is attacked and murdered on the staircase in *Psycho*, even though the build-up to the moment has been loaded with disquiet, even though the audience knows that something terrible is about to happen, from the gloom of the old house, the sinister appearance of the high staircase, the apprehension on the actor's face – the shock when it comes is so sudden that audiences cried out in terror, and as a release.

The other principal element that Hitchcock has invested with a unique flavour is sex. His approach has been copied by other directors to the point where it has become a cliché. The Hitchcock heroine often falls into the stereotype of the composed, aloof blonde, making plain by her attitude disinterest or antipathy towards the hero, but somehow simultaneously luring him on. Ambiguity is again apparent – sometimes the hero doesn't know which side she is on, as in *North by Northwest*, or has cause to despise the girl, as in *Notorious* or *The Birds*. Women quite often are made to suffer outrageous torment in Hitchcock films – Ingrid Bergman is slowly poisoned in *Notorious* and *Under Capricorn*, Edna Best and Doris Day lose their children to kidnappers in the two versions of *The Man Who Knew Too Much*, Tippi Hedren in *The Birds* and *Marnie* and Vera Miles in *The Wrong Man* go out of their

Jon Finch, Anna Massey and Clive Swift in *Frenzy*, Hitchcock's 52nd feature film and his first made in England for more than twenty years

minds, Tallulah Bankhead loses all her material possessions in *Lifeboat*, Janet Leigh in *Psycho* and many other beautiful victims in other films are brutally murdered. Of these the Tallulah character is significant, for she emerges from her ordeal a conspicuously better person, purged of the arrogance and cynicism that made her initially unsympathetic. There is, it seems, a fundamental distrust of women and a need to bring them to an acceptable standard. Is this attitude, too, part of the Jesuit upbringing? It is interesting that the actors he prefers are those with a screen personality so strong that it is often larger than the role they are playing. The identification of the audience is more complete when it is watching James Stewart or Cary Grant, both of whom made four appearances in Hitchcock leads, than it is with less engaging performers.

Alfred Hitchcock made his name in films at an early age. And he kept it, increasing his stature as a film-maker as the years went on. The perfectionism and skill coupled with the monumental cinematic imagination have brought a lasting, major contribution to the art of the film, and if his genius has been decried on the absurd grounds that too many people enjoy his work on an uncritical level, then his contribution to the enrichment of humankind should not go unremarked either. That is and always has been his intention – to entertain the widest possible audience. Beyond his films, which he will publicize as ruthlessly as a P. T. Barnum, using his forceful personality to the utmost in the task, he is a modest, quiet-living man, not given to exaggerated or unorthodox behaviour beyond a sly penchant for practical joking.

He spends much of his days now in his house up the California coast between San Francisco and Los Angeles, supervising his creative work from the bungalow office complex on the lot at Universal City. His Los Angeles home backs on to the Bel Air golf course. He has been contentedly married to Alma Reville for nearly fifty years and they have one daughter, Patricia, who before her marriage briefly embarked on an acting career and can be seen in a small role in *Stage Fright* and a rather larger one in *Strangers on a Train*. His tastes are conservative – he has rows of identically cut dark blue suits, and when in Europe always stays in London at Claridge's and in Switzerland at the Palace Hotel, St Moritz. In spite of all the years in America his voice has never lost its London twang, which he has retained almost deliberately as another device for gaining instant audience recognition.

He is a classless figure, his appeal is universal in every sense. He is without doubt the greatest film director to emerge from within the British industry, and it is a matter for pride, and some surprise, that he was able, within the poor system that prevailed there between the wars, to bring to it a very special lustre, which coupled with his greater contribution to the American cinema, will be his enduring memorial.

Hitchcock Filmography

1921–1922 Wrote and designed titles:

Call of Youth
The Great Day
The Princess of New York
Bonnie Briar Bush
Tell Your Children
Three Live Gosts
Mystery Road
Dangerous Lives
The Spanish Jade

1921 **Number Thirteen** (Unfinished)
W. and F. *Producer, director*: Alfred Hitchcock.
Photographer: Rosenthal. *Leading players*: Clare
Greet, Ernest Thesiger

Always Tell Your Wife
(Completed with Seymour Hicks when original
director fell ill)

Woman to Woman
Balcon–Saville–Freedman. *P* Michael Balcon.
D Graham Cutts. *S* Cutts, Hitchcock. *Ph* Claude
L. McDonnell. *Asst. dir, design*: Hitchcock.
Lp Betty Compson, Clive Brook

1923 **The White Shadow**
Balcon–Saville–Freedman. *P* Michael Balcon.
D Graham Cutts. *S* Michael Morton, Hitchcock.
Asst. dir, design: Hitchcock. *Lp* Betty Compson,
Clive Brook

1924 **The Passionate Adventure**
Gainsborough. *P* Michael Balcon. *D* Graham
Cutts. *S* Hitchcock, Michael Morton. *Asst. dir,
design*: Hitchcock. *Lp* Clive Brook, Lillian
Hall-Davies

1925 **The Blackguard**
Gainsborough. *P* Michael Balcon. *D* Graham
Cutts. *S* Hitchcock. *Asst. dir, design*: Hitchcock.
Lp Walter Rilla, Jane Novak

The Prude's Fall
Balcon–Saville–Freedman. *P* Michael Balcon.
D Graham Cutts. *S* Hitchcock. *Asst. dir, design*:
Hitchcock. *Lp* Betty Compson

The Pleasure Garden
Gainsborough. *P* Michael Balcon. *S* Eliot
Stannard. *Ph* Baron Ventimiglia. *Lp* Virginia
Valli, Carmelita Geraghty, Miles Mander, John
Stuart

1926 **The Mountain Eagle** (U.S. *Fear O' God*)
Gainsborough. *P* Michael Balcon. *S* Eliot
Stannard. *Ph* Baron Ventimiglia. *Lp* Nita Naldi,
Malcolm Keen

The Lodger
Gainsborough. *P* Michael Balcon.
S Hitchcock, Eliot Stannard, from novel by

Mrs Belloc-Lowndes. *Ph* Baron Ventimiglia.
Titles: Ivor Montagu. *Lp* Ivor Novello, June,
Marie Ault, Malcolm Keen, Arthur Chesney

1927 **Downhill** (U.S. *When Boys Leave Home*)
Gainsborough. *P* Michael Balcon. *S* Eliot
Stannard, from play by Ivor Novello and
Constance Collier. *Ph* Claude L. McDonnell.
Lp Ivor Novello, Robin Irvine, Lillian
Braithwaite, Ben Webster, Violet Farebrother,
Isabel Jeans, Ian Hunter

Easy Virtue
Gainsborough. *P* Michael Balcon. *S* Eliot
Stannard, from play by Noël Coward. *Ph* Claude
L. McDonnell. *Ed* Ivor Montagu. *Lp* Isabel
Jeans, Franlyn Dyall, Bransby Williams, Ian
Hunter, Robin Irvine, Violet Farebrother

The Ring
B.I.P. *P* John Maxwell. *S* Hitchcock. *Ph* Jack
Cox. *Lp* Carl Brisson, Lillian Hall-Davies, Ian
Hunter, Harry Terry, Gordon Harker, Forrester
Harvey, Billy Wells

1928 **The Farmer's Wife**
B.I.P. *P* John Maxwell. *S* Hitchcock, from play
by Eden Philpotts. *Ph* Jack Cox. *Lp* Jameson
Thomas, Lillian Hall-Davies, Gordon Harker,
Maud Gill, Louise Pounds, Olga Slade, Antonia
Brough

Champagne
B.I.P. *P* John Maxwell. *S* Eliot Stannard.
Ph Jack Cox. *Lp* Betty Balfour, Gordon Harker,
Jack Trevor, Ferdinand von Alten, Marcel
Vibert, Jean Bradin

1929 **The Manxman**
B.I.P. *P* John Maxwell. *S* Eliot Stannard (from
novel by Hall Caine). *Ph* Jack Cox. *Lp* Carl
Brisson, Malcolm Keen, Anny Ondra, Randle
Ayrton, Clare Greet

Sound:
Blackmail
B.I.P. *P* John Maxwell. *S* Hitchcock, Benn W.
Levy, Charles Bennett. *Ph* Jack Cox. *M* Hubert
Bath, Henry Stafford. *Lp* Anny Ondra, John
Longden, Sara Allgood, Charles Paton, Donald
Calthrop, Cyril Ritchard, Hannah Jones, Harvey
Braban, Phyllis Monkman

1930 **Elstree Calling**
B.I.P. *supervising director*: Adrian Brunel.
Hitchcock contributed two sequences

Juno and the Paycock
B.I.P. *P* John Maxwell. *S* Hitchcock, Alma
Reville, from play by Sean O'Casey. *Ph* Jack
Cox. *Lp* Barry Fitzgerald, Sara Allgood, Edward
Chapman, Marie O'Neill, Sidney Morgan, John
Laurie, Dennis Wyndham, John Longden,
Kathleen O'Regan, Dave Morris, Fred Schwartz

Murder
B.I.P. *P* John Maxwell. *S* Alma Revill, from play
by Clemence Dane and Helen Simpson. *Ph* Jack
Cox. *Lp* Herbert Marshall, Norah Baring, Phyllis
Konstam, Edward Chapman, Miles Mander,
Esme Chaplin, A. Brandon Thomas, Joynson
Powell, Esme Percy, Donald Calthrop, Clare
Greet

1931 The Skin Game
B.I.P. *P* John Maxwell. *S* Hitchcock, Alma
Reville, from play by John Galsworthy. *Ph* Jack
Cox. *Lp* Edmund Gwenn, Jill Esmond, John
Longden, C. V. France, Helen Haye, Phyllis
Konstam, Frank Lawton, Herbert Ross, Dora
Gregory, Edward Chapman, Ronald Frankau,
R. E. Jeffrey, George Blanchof

1932 Rich and Strange (U.S. *East of Shanghai*)
B.I.P. *P* John Maxwell. *S* Alma Reville, Val
Valentine (from story by Dale Collins). *Ph* Jack
Cox, Charles Martin. *Lp* Henry Kendall, Joan
Barry, Betty Amann, Percy Marmont, Elsie
Randolph

Number Seventeen
B.I.P. *P* John Maxwell. *S* Hitchcock, Alma
Reville, Rodney Ackland (from play by Jefferson
Farjeon). *Ph* Jack Cox, Bryan Langley. *Lp* Leon
M. Lion, Anne Grey, John Stuart, Donald
Calthrop, Barry Jones, Gary Marsh, Henry Caine

Lord Camber's Ladies
B.I.P. *P* Alfred Hitchcock. *D* Benn W. Levy.
Lp Gertrude Lawrence, Gerald du Maurier

1933 Waltzes from Vienna (U.S. *Strauss's Great Waltz*)
P Tom Arnold. *S* Alma Reville, Guy Botton.
Ph Glen McWilliams. *M* Johann Strauss Sr and
Jr, adapted by Hubert Bath. *Lp* Jessie Matthews,
Esmond Knight, Frank Vosper, Edmund Gwenn,
Fay Compton, Robert Hale

1934 The Man Who Knew Too Much
Gaumont-British. *P* Michael Balcon, Ivor
Montagu. *S* A. R. Rawlinson, Edwin
Greenwood, from story by Charles Bennett,
D. B. Wyndham-Lewis. *Ph* Curt Courant.
M Arthur Benjamin, Louis Levy. *Lp* Leslie
Banks, Peter Lorre, Edna Best, Nova Pilbeam,
Hugh Wakefield, Pierre Fresnay, Frank Vosper

1935 The Thirty-Nine Steps
Gaumont-British. *P* Michael Balcon, Ivor
Montagu. *S* Charles Bennett, Ian Hay, from
novel by John Buchan. *Ph* Bernard Knowles.
M Louis Levy. *Lp* Robert Donat, Madeleine
Carroll, Lucie Mannheim, Godfrey Tearle, John
Laurie, Peggy Ashcroft, Frank Cellier, Wylie
Watson, Peggy Simpson, Gus McNaughton,
Jerry Verno

1936 The Secret Agent
Gaumont-British. *P* Michael Balcon, Ivor
Montagu. *S* Charles Bennett, from play by
Campbell Dixon based on Somerset Maugham's
novel *Ashenden*. *Ph* Bernard Knowles. *M* Louis
Levy. *Lp* Madeleine Carroll, John Geilgud, Peter
Lorre, Robert Young, Percy Marmont, Florence
Kohn, Lilli Palmer, Charles Carson

Sabotage (U.S. *A Woman Alone*)
Gaumont-British. *P* Michael Balcon, Ivor
Montagu. *S* Charles Bennett, after novel by
Joseph Conrad. *Ph* Bernard Knowles. *M* Louis
Levy. *Lp* Sylvia Sidney, Oscar Homolka,
Desmond Tester, John Loder, Joyce Barbour,
Matthew Boulton, S. J. Warmington, William
Dewhurst, Peter Bull, Torin Thatcher, Austin
Trevor, Clare Greet, Sam Wilkinson, Sara
Allgood, Martita Hunt, Pamela Bevan

1937 Young and Innocent (U.S. *The Girl Was Young*)
Gainsborough. *P* Edward Black. *S* Charles
Bennett, from novel by Josephine Tey.
Ph Bernard Knowles. *M* Louis Levy. *Lp* Derrick
de Marney, Nova Pilbeam, Percy Marmont,
Edward Rigby, Mary Clare, John Longden,
George Curzon, Basil Radford, Pamela Carne,
Jerry Verno, Torin Thatcher, Peggy Simpson,
Anna Konstam

1938 The Lady Vanishes
Gainsborough. *P* Edward Black. *S* Sidney
Gilliatt, Frank Launder, from the novel by Ethel
Lina White. *Ph* Jack Cox. *M* Louis Levy.
Lp Michael Redgrave, Margaret Lockwood, Paul
Lukas, Dame May Whitty, Googie Withers,
Cecil Parker, Linden Travers, Mary Clare,
Naunton Wayne, Basil Radford, Catherine Lacey

1939 Jamaica Inn
Mayflower. *P* Erich Pommer, Charles Laughton.
S Sidney Gilliatt, Joan Harrison, from novel by
Daphne du Maurier. *Ph* Harry Stradling, Bernard
Knowles. *M* Eric Fenby. *Lp* Charles Laughton,
Maureen O'Hara, Robert Newton, Emlyn
Williams, Leslie Banks, Horace Hodges, Hay
Petrie, Frederick Piper, Marie Ney, Wylie
Watson, Morland Graham, Edwin Greenwood,
Mervyn Johns, Stephen Haggard, Herbert
Lomas, Clare Greet, William Devlin, Basil
Radford, Jeanne de Casalis

1940 U.S.A.

✶ Rebecca
Selznick–UA. *P* David O. Selznick. *S* Robert
E. Sherwood, Joan Harrison. *Ph* George Barnes.
M Franz Waxman. *Lp* Laurence Olivier, Joan
Fontaine, George Sanders, Judith Anderson,
Nigel Bruce, Reginald Denny, C. Aubrey Smith,
Gladys Cooper, Florence Bates, Melville Cooper,
Leo G. Carroll, Leonard Carey, Lumsden Hare,
Edward Fielding, Philip Winter, Forrester
Harvey

Foreign Correspondent
United Artists. *P* Walter Wanger. *S* Charles
Bennett, Joan Harrison. *Ph* Rudolph Maté.
M Alfred Newman. *Lp* Joel McCrea, Laraine
Day, Herbert Marshall, George Sanders, Albert
Bassermann, Robert Benchley, Edmund Gwenn,
Harry Davenport, Eduardo Ciannelli, Martin
Kosleck, Jane Novak

1941 Mr and Mrs Smith
RKO. *P* Harry Edington. *S* Norman Krasna.
Ph Harry Stradling. *M* Roy Webb. *Lp* Carole
Lombard, Robert Montgomery, Gene Raymond,
Jack Carson, Philip Merivale, Lucile Watson,
William Tracey, Charles Halton, Esther Dale,
Emma Dunn, Betty Compson

Suspicion
RKO. *S* Samson Raphaelson, Joan Harrison,
Alma Reville, from novel by Francis Iles.
Ph Harry Stradling. *M* Franz Waxman. *Lp* Cary
Grant, Joan Fontaine, Cedric Hardwicke, Nigel
Bruce, Dame May Whitty, Isabel Jeans, Heather
Angel, Auriol Lee, Reginald Sheffield, Leo G.
Carroll

1942 Saboteur
Universal. *P* Frank Lloyd, Jack H. Skirball.
S Peter Viertel, Joan Harrison, Dorothy Parker.

Ph Joseph Valentine. M Charles Previn. Lp Robert Cummings, Priscilla Lane, Otto Kruger, Norman Lloyd, Alan Baxter, Clem Bevans, Alma Kruger, Vaughan Glazer, Dorothy Petersen, Murray Alper

1943 **Shadow of a Doubt**
Universal. P Jack H. Skirball. S Thornton Wilder, Alma Reville, Sally Benson, from story by Gordon McDonnell. Ph Joseph Valentine. M Dmitri Tiomkin. Lp Joseph Cotten, Teresa Wright, MacDonald Carey, Henry Travers, Patricia Collinge, Hume Cronyn, Wallace Ford, Charles Bates, Edna May Wonacott, Irving Bacon

Lifeboat
Twentieth Century-Fox. P Kenneth MacGowan. S Jo Swerling, from story by John Steinbeck. Ph Glen MacWilliams. M Hugo Friedhofer. Lp Tallulah Bankhead, William Bendix, Walter Slezak, Mary Anderson, John Hodiak, Henry Hull, Heather Angel, Hume Cronyn, Canada Lee

1944 **Bon Voyage** (U.K.)
Ministry of Information. S J. O. C. Orton, Angus McPhail, from original story by Arthur Calder-Marshall. Ph Gunther Krampf. Lp John Blythe, the Molière Players

Aventure Malgache (U.K.)
Ministry of Information. S J. O. C. Orton, Angus McPhail. Ph Gunther Krampf. Lp The Molière Players

1945 **Spellbound**
Selznick International. P David O. Selznick. S Ben Hecht, from novel by Francis Beeding. Ph George Barnes. M Miklos Rozsa. Dream sequence: Salvador Dali. Lp Ingrid Bergman, Gregory Peck, Michael Chekhov, Jean Acker, Donald Curtis, Rhonda Fleming, John Emery, Leo G. Carroll, Norman Lloyd, Steven Geray, Paul Harvey, Erskine Sanford, Janet Scott, Victor Kilian, Wallace Ford, Regis Toomey

1946 **Notorious**
RKO. P Hitchcock. S Ben Hecht, from original story by Hitchcock. Ph Ted Tetzlaff. M Roy Webb. Lp Cary Grant, Ingrid Bergman, Claude Rains, Louis Calhern, Leopoldine Konstantin, Reinhold Schuntzel, Moroni Olsen, Ivan Triesault, Alex Minotis, Wally Brown, Sir Charles Mendl, Lenore Ulric

1947 **The Paradine Case**
Selznick International. P David O. Selznick. S David O. Selznick, from novel by Robert Hichens. Ph Lee Garmes. M Franz Waxman. Lp Gregory Peck, Charles Laughton, Ann Todd, Charles Coburn, Ethel Barrymore, Louis Jourdan, Alida Valli, Leo G. Carroll, Joan Tetzel, John Goldsworthy, Lester Matthews, Pat Aherne, Colin Hunter, Isobel Elsom, John Williams

1948 **Rope**
Transatlantic. P Hitchcock, Sidney Bernstein. S Arthur Laurents, from play by Patrick Hamilton. Ph Joseph Valentine, William V. Skell. Technicolor. M Leo. F. Forbstein, based on Poulenc theme. Lp James Stewart, John Dall, Farley Granger, Joan Chandler, Sir Cedric Hardwick, Constance Collier, Douglas Dick, Edith Evanston, Dick Hogan.

1949 **Under Capricorn** (U.K.)
Transatlantic. P Hitchcock, Sidney Bernstein. S James Bridie, from novel by Helen Simpson. Ph Jack Cardiff. Technicolor. M Richard Addinsell. Lp Ingrid Bergman, Joseph Cotten, Michael Wilding, Margaret Leighton, Cecil Parker, Denis O'Dea, Jack Watling, Harcourt Williams, John Ruddock, Bill Shine, Victor Lucas, Ronald Adam, Francis de Wolff, S. H. Mulcaster, Olive Sloane, Maureen Delaney, Julia Lang, Betty McDermott, Roderick Lovell

1950 **Stage Fright** (U.K.)
A.B.P.C. P Hitchcock, Fred Ahern. S Whitfield Cook, from stories by Selwyn Jepson. Ph Wilkie Cooper. M Leighton Lucas. Lp Marlene Dietrich, Jane Wyman, Michael Wilding, Richard Todd, Alastair Sim, Sybil Thorndike, Kay Walsh, Miles Malleson, Hector MacGregor, Joyce Grenfell, André Morell, Patricia Hitchcock

1951 **Strangers on a Train**
Warner. P Hitchcock. S Raymond Chandler, Czenzi Ormonde, from novel by Patricia Highsmith. Ph Robert Burks. M Dmitri Tiomkin. Lp Robert Walker, Farley Granger, Ruth Roman, Leo G. Carroll, Patricia Hitchcock, Laura Elliott, Marion Lorne, Jonathan Hale, Howard St John, John Brown, Norma Varden

1952 **I Confess**
Warner. P Hitchcock. S George Tabori, William Archibald, from play by Paul Anthelme. Ph Robert Burks. M Dmitri Tiomkin. Lp Montgomery Clift, Anne Baxter, Karl Malden, Brian Aherne, O. E. Hasse, Roger Dann, Dolly Haas, Charles Andre, Judson Pratt, Ovila Legare, Gilles Pelletier

1954 **Dial M for Murder**
Warner. P Hitchcock. S Frederick Knott, from his play. Ph Robert Burks. Warnercolor and 3-D. M Dmitri Tiomkin. Lp Ray Milland, Grace Kelly, Robert Cummings, John Williams, Anthony Dawson, Lee Britt, Patrick Allan, George Leigh, George Alderson, Robin Hughes

Rear Window
Paramount. P Hitchcock. S John Michael Hayes, from story by Cornell Woolrich. Ph Robert Burks. Technicolor. M Franz Waxman. Lp James Stewart, Grace Kelly, Wendell Corey, Thelma Ritter, Raymond Burr, Judith Evelyn, Ross Bagdasarian, Georgine Darcy, Jesslyn Fox, Rand Harper, Irene Winston, Sara Berner, Frank Cady

1955 **To Catch a Thief**
Paramount. P Hitchcock. S John Michael Hayes, from novel by David Dodge. Ph Robert Burks. Technicolor and VistaVision. M Lynn Murray. Lp Cary Grant, Grace Kelly, Jessie Royce Landis, John Williams, Charles Vanel, Brigitte Auber, Jean Martinelli, René Blancard

1956 **The Trouble with Harry**
Paramount. P Hitchcock. S John Michael Hayes, from novel by Jack Trevor Story. Ph Robert Burks. Technicolor and VistaVision. M Bernard Herrman. Lp Edmund Gwenn, John Forsythe,

Shirley Maclaine, Mildred Natwick, Mildred Dunnock, Jerry Mathers, Royal Dano, Parker Fernelly, Barry Macollum

The Man Who Knew Too Much
Filwite Productions–Paramount. *P* Hitchcock. *S* John Michael Hayes, Angus McPhail, from original story by Charles Bennett and D. B. Wyndham-Lewis. *Ph* Robert Burks. Technicolor and VistaVision. *M* Bernard Herrman. *Lp* James Stewart, Doris Day, Brenda de Banzie, Bernard Miles, Ralph Truman, Daniel Gelin, Mogens Wieth, Alan Mowbray, Hillary Brooke, Christopher Olsen, Reggie Nalder, Richard Wattis, Betty Beskomb, Carolyn Jones, Patrick Aherne

1957 **The Wrong Man**
Warner. *P* Hitchcock. *S* Maxwell Anderson, Angus McPhail. *Ph* Robert Burks. *M* Bernard Herrman. *Lp* Henry Fonda, Vera Miles, Anthony Quayle, Harold J. Stone, Charles Cooper, John Heldabrand, Esther Minciotti, Richard Robbins

1958 **Vertigo**
Paramount. *P* Hitchcock. *S* Alec Cooper, Samuel Taylor, from novel by Pierre Boileau and Thomas Narcejac. *Ph* Robert Burks. Technicolor and VistaVision. *M* Bernard Herrman. *Lp* James Stewart, Kim Novak, Barbara Bell Geddes, Henry Jones, Tom Helmore, Raymond Bailey, Ellen Corby, Lee Patrick, Konstantin Shayne

1959 **North by Northwest**
MGM. *P* Hitchcock. *S* Ernest Lehmen. *Ph* Robert Burks. Technicolor and VistaVision. *M* Bernard Herrman. *Lp* Cary Grant, Eva Marie Saint, James Mason, Jessie Royce Landis, Leo G. Carroll, Philip Ober, Josephine Hutchinson, Martin Landau, Adam Williams, Edward Platt

1960 **Psycho**
Paramount. *P* Hitchcock. *S* Joseph Stefans, from novel by Robert Bloch. *Ph* John L. Russell. *M* Bernard Herrman. *Lp* Anthony Perkins, Janet Leigh, Vera Miles, John Gavin, Martin Balsam, John McIntyre, Simon Oakland

1963 **The Birds**
Universal. *P* Hitchcock. *S* Evan Hunter, from story by Daphne du Maurier. *Ph* Robert Burks. Technicolor. *Sound consultant*: Bernard Herrman. *Lp* Rod Taylor, Tippi Hedren, Jessica Tandy, Suzanne Pleshette, Veronica Cartwright, Ethel Griffies, Charles McGraw

1964 **Marnie**
Universal. *P* Hitchcock. *S* J. Presson Allen, from novel by Winston Graham. *Ph* Robert Burks. Technicolor. *Lp* Tippi Hedren, Sean Connery, Diane Baker, Louise Lotham, Alan Napier, Martin Gabel, Mariette Hartley, Bruce Dern

1966 **Torn Curtain**
Universal. *P* Hitchcock. *S* Brian Moore. *Ph* John F. Warren. Technicolor. *M* John Addison. *Lp* Paul Newman, Julie Andrews, Lila Kedrova, Hansjöerg Felmy, Tamara Toumenova, Wolfgang Kieling, Günter Strack, Ludwig Donath, David Opatoshu, Gisela Fisher, Mort Mills, Carolyn Conwell, Arthur Gould-Porter

1970 **Topaz**
Universal. *P* Hitchcock. *S* Samuel Taylor, from novel by Leon Uris. *Ph* Jack Hildyard. Technicolor. *M* Maurice Jarré. *Lp* Frederick Stafford, John Forsythe, Karin Dor, Dany Robin, John Vernon, Michel Piccoli, Philippe Noiret, Claude Jade, Michel Subor, Roscoe Lee-Browne, Per-Axel Arosenius

1972 **Frenzy**
Universal. *P* Hitchcock. *S* Anthony Shaffer, from novel by Arthur Le Bern. *Ph* Gil Taylor. *M* Ron Goodwin. *Lp* Barry Foster, Jon Finch, Alec McCowen, Anna Massey, Barbara Leigh-Hunt, Vivien Merchant, Bernard Cribbins, Billie Whitelaw, Michael Bates, Jimmy Gardner, Rita Webb, Clive Swift

Books about Alfred Hitchcock in English

Francois Truffaut *Hitchcock* Simon and Schuster, New York 1967 and Secker and Warburg, London 1968

Robin Wood *Hitchcock's Films* Zwemmer, London and Barnes, New York 1965, revised 1969

George Perry *The Films of Alfred Hitchcock* Studio Vista, London and E. P. Dutton, New York 1965

Focus on Hitchcock Edited by Albert J. LaValley Prentice-Hall, New Jersey 1972

Raymond Durgnat *The Strange Case of Alfred Hitchcock* Faber, London 1974

Index

Acknowledgments

Most of the stills in this book are from the National Film Archive. The colour pictures are from the John Kobal Collection. Thanks are due to Cinema International Corporation Ltd, Columbia–Warner Ltd and the Rank Organisation for the use of stills of their films.
Thanks are also due to Nancy J. Buquoi for creative assistance and to Catherine Gurr for typing the index and filmography.